THE COMPLETE
IDIOT'S
GUIDE® TO

Overcoming Procrastination

Second Edition

by Michelle Tullier, PhD

ALPHA

A member of Penguin Group (USA) Inc.

For Alexandra "I'll clean my room tomorrow" Gazelle.

ALPHA BOOKS

Published by Penguin Group (USA) Inc.

Penguin Group (USA) Inc., 375 Hudson Street, New York, New York 10014, USA • Penguin Group (Canada), 90 Eglinton Avenue East, Suite 700, Toronto, Ontario M4P 2Y3, Canada (a division of Pearson Penguin Canada Inc.) • Penguin Books Ltd., 80 Strand, London WC2R 0RL, England • Penguin Ireland, 25 St. Stephen's Green, Dublin 2, Ireland (a division of Penguin Books Ltd.) • Penguin Group (Australia), 250 Camberwell Road, Camberwell, Victoria 3124, Australia (a division of Pearson Australia Group Pty. Ltd.) • Penguin Books India Pvt. Ltd., 11 Community Centre, Panchsheel Park, New Delhi—110 017, India • Penguin Group (NZ), 67 Apollo Drive, Rosedale, North Shore, Auckland 1311, New Zealand (a division of Pearson New Zealand Ltd.) • Penguin Books (South Africa) (Pty.) Ltd., 24 Sturdee Avenue, Rosebank, Johannesburg 2196, South Africa • Penguin Books Ltd., Registered Offices: 80 Strand, London WC2R 0RL, England

Copyright © 2012 by Michelle Tullier, PhD

International Standard Book Number: 978-1-61564-211-3
Library of Congress Catalog Card Number: 2012903083

14   8   7   6   5   4   3

Interpretation of the printing code: The rightmost number of the first series of numbers is the year of the book's printing; the rightmost number of the second series of numbers is the number of the book's printing. For example, a printing code of 12-1 shows that the first printing occurred in 2012.

Printed in the United States of America

Note: This publication contains the opinions and ideas of its author. It is intended to provide helpful and informative material on the subject matter covered. It is sold with the understanding that the author and publisher are not engaged in rendering professional services in the book. If the reader requires personal assistance or advice, a competent professional should be consulted.

The author and publisher specifically disclaim any responsibility for any liability, loss, or risk, personal or otherwise, which is incurred as a consequence, directly or indirectly, of the use and application of any of the contents of this book.

Most Alpha books are available at special quantity discounts for bulk purchases for sales promotions, premiums, fund-raising, or educational use. Special books, or book excerpts, can also be created to fit specific needs. For details, write: Special Markets, Alpha Books, 375 Hudson Street, New York, NY 10014.

Publisher: *Mike Sanders*
Executive Managing Editor: *Billy Fields*
Senior Acquisitions Editor: *Brook Farling*
Development Editor: *Ginny Bess Munroe*
Senior Production Editor: *Kayla Dugger*
Copy Editor: *Jan Zoya*

Cover Designer: *Rebecca Batchelor*
Book Designers: *William Thomas, Rebecca Batchelor*
Indexer: *Celia McCoy*
Layout: *Brian Massey*
Senior Proofreader: *Laura Caddell*

Contents

Introduction

How many things were you supposed to do yesterday that didn't get done? How likely are you to do them today? Tomorrow? Okay, how about if I give you until next week? Can you have them done by then?

Wait! Don't close the book yet! I know those are annoying questions, but I had to ask. As a recovering procrastinator myself, I know what the secret life of a procrastinator is like. You go through each day hoping no one will discover how far behind you are on projects at work, how much mold is growing on the leftovers in the back of your fridge, or how long it's been since you wrote to your Great-Aunt Norma in Salinas.

This book is your chance to come clean, to admit to yourself and others that you've developed a habit of putting things off, not finishing what you start, and doing things at the last minute. Don't worry; you'll be in good company. As you'll see from the real-life examples and quotes in this book, just about everybody procrastinates, either occasionally or chronically. It's become something of an epidemic as life has become more complicated, thanks to technological, workplace, and societal changes (which I describe in Chapter 1).

Drawing from my knowledge base of a doctorate in psychology, my experience as a career and life-planning counselor, my many years as a facilitator of procrastination and time-management seminars, plus conversations with hundreds of procrastinators from all walks of life, I bring you practical, painless, easy-to-implement solutions to the problem. You'll learn why you procrastinate, how to break the habit, and how to keep it broken.

Most important, you'll learn that the key to being productive is not just to do more and more like some sort of time-management robot, but to focus instead on doing what's important to you and to the people you care about, while having plenty of fun along the way.

In this book, I show you how to stop putting off things like cleaning out your closet, preparing your taxes, making a career change, and much more. But through it all, I urge you to enjoy life when you can, relax a little, and stop to smell the basil.

How to Use This Book

Procrastinators are famous for wanting to skip around in books rather than methodically plod through them from page 1 to the end. Though I recommend that you try to read the chapters at least roughly in order, skipping around isn't such a bad thing if that's the quickest route to the answers you need. To that end, here's a brief overview of what's inside:

Part 1, The Whats, Whys, and Woes of Procrastination, helps you get your bearings. It wakes you up to the dangers of procrastination so that you'll be motivated to break the habit. And it tells you what procrastination is and why it's so common. You'll also find chapters that help you pinpoint the reasons why you put off things and a chapter on why your past efforts to get over the problem haven't worked and how you will be able to overcome procrastination this time.

Part 2, The Path to Becoming an Ex-Procrastinator, provides the foundation for solving your problem. There's a special focus on getting rid of clutter, becoming organized, simplifying your life, and learning to make decisions. These steps play an important role in overcoming procrastination. The final chapter of this part lets you in on the "prescription" for overcoming procrastination in any area of your life.

Part 3, Let's Get It Done (Already), is the nitty-gritty, down-and-dirty part of the book. In these chapters, I roll up my sleeves and help you get those dishes washed, keep your New Year's resolutions, and stop putting off home repair projects or doctors' appointments. You'll find tips for taking care of to-do lists and reaching goals related to your life at home, work, school, online, and socially. You'll also learn how to attend to your health, wealth, safety, and, most important, happiness. This part concludes with words of wisdom for ensuring you stay on track as an ex-procrastinator.

Extras

To highlight special tips and resources, useful facts, pitfalls to watch out for, and insights from fellow procrastinators, there are sidebars scattered throughout each chapter. You can spot them by their icons, which are as follows:

ACTION TACTIC

These are snippets of advice to act on immediately or quick tips to get you moving and soaring toward your goals.

QUICKSAND!

Read these for alerts to pitfalls and common mistakes that might have you stuck in a rut, unable to take action.

MATTER OF FACT

These sidebars clue you in to interesting or fun bits of information and direct you to books, websites, organizations, and other resources that can help you get things done.

YOU'RE NOT ALONE

These are quotes and anecdotes from real people talking about their procrastination problems, insights from experts, and words of wisdom from famous or historical figures.

Acknowledgments

Even the author of a book on overcoming procrastination needs help getting past writer's block, meeting deadlines, and maintaining some degree of sanity in her life. Many people had a hand in making those things happen.

Thank you to my remarkable daughter, Alexandra, for letting my writing take center stage for a while, as it has too many times in your 14 years. Thank you to the many Facebook friends whose words of encouragement—from the heartfelt, to the sage and practical, to the just plain goofy—kept me motivated and laughing. Thank you to my LinkedIn and Facebook networks for your helpful responses to my procrastination survey.

My gratitude also goes to the many friends and colleagues, including Sally Dougan, Leslie Kuban, and Tim Haft, as well as those quoted anonymously, who shared their own useful tips, knowledge, or personal struggles with procrastination.

Special thanks to Ellen Sautter for just-in-time stats and knowledge-sharing on social networking, and to John Walker for his skillful technical review of the oh-so-serious parts. And thank you to Lisa George and Molly Minnear for always being there with bells on.

I am also very grateful to my top-notch editing team, Ginny Bess Munroe, Kayla Dugger, and Jan Zoya, and to Acquisitions Editor Brook Farling for making a second edition happen. You all bring out the best in an author.

Trademarks

The Whats, Whys, and Woes of Procrastination

So you've gotten this far. You've bought, borrowed, or begged for this book. You've vowed to do something about your procrastination problem once and for all. Congratulations!

But are you already concerned that you won't finish the book and make some real changes in your life? Well, worry no longer! These first four chapters will show you that procrastination is not a permanent character flaw or an addiction you can't crack. Instead, it is something you can figure out, psych out, and snuff out.

In the first chapter, you'll learn what procrastination is—besides that nagging feeling in your stomach reminding you of all the things you ought to be doing. And you'll see how widespread a problem procrastination is and why it's a habit that needs to be broken. In Chapter 2 and Chapter 3, you explore the causes of procrastination so you can start to root it out at its source.

Then, just when you might be starting to worry that it's too big of a problem to conquer, Chapter 4 will help you understand how successful changes are made and why you really will be able to overcome procrastination this go-around.

Why We Procrastinate and Why It's a Problem

In This Chapter

- What it means to procrastinate
- Why procrastination is a growing problem
- Why we love to hate and hate to love doing it
- Why procrastination is sometimes a good thing
- The toll procrastination takes on your health, wealth, and happiness

You know the feeling. It's that sense of dread or even panic that comes when you realize you haven't gotten around to starting something you should be doing or haven't finished something that should've been crossed off your list long ago. It comes from those untouched projects closing in on you around the house or that report your boss is expecting tomorrow that you should've started yesterday. Maybe it's the exam you're going to have to stay up all night cramming for because you've been working really hard to get the last word in Words with Friends.

Adding insult to injury is probably a backlog of unanswered email and voice mail, boxes that haven't been unpacked from your last three moves, and the New Year's resolution to lose weight that succumbed to a pepperoni pizza on January 3. Face it: you're a procrastinator.

The Procrastination Epidemic— You're Not Alone!

Procrastination is everywhere, and everybody does it, either chronically or occasionally. According to research published recently in the journal of the *American Psychological Association*, 26 percent of Americans consider themselves to be chronic procrastinators, up significantly from 5 percent in the 1970s. And research from various sources over the years has consistently shown that at least 90 to 95 percent of people report that they procrastinate occasionally.

With life on this planet getting more complicated every day and offering more distractions, procrastination is becoming something of an epidemic. Technological advances, changes in the workplace, and the evolution of family or home life have made people feel overwhelmed, overextended, and resentful of all they are supposed to be doing or think they should be doing. There's more for us to do and higher expectations for when we'll get it all done.

Technology: Timesaver or Timewaster?

Remember what life was like when all you had to deal with was one email box? Never mind those of us old enough to remember life before email at all! Now we get bombarded from so many angles— text messages on our phones; email in our personal, work, and school mailboxes; LinkedIn messages; Facebook chats; comments on our blogs; Twitter followers waiting for our next 140 characters of wisdom; and much more. Everyone expects us to respond or take action, and they expect it almost instantaneously.

Then there are the ways technology helps us kill time so beautifully. Between apps, games, gadgets, Google doodles, and gizmos on our smart phones, tablets, laptops, desktops, Xboxes, and TVs, we're almost never without enticing distractions leading us into the temptation of procrastination.

ACTION TACTIC

Try designating one day a month or even just part of a day as a technology-free time zone. You might not be able to give up your mobile phone if it's your lifeline to the world, but try using it only for old-fashioned calls instead of texting, using apps, or going online. And don't use your computer, tablet, gaming devices, television, or other electronic gadgets. Give yourself a break from the pressure of being constantly in touch with the world and a chance to get other things done.

How Work Overload Fuels Procrastination

Unless you've been living under a rock for the past several years (which procrastinators sometimes feel like they're doing), you've no doubt heard about or experienced the dramatic changes that have taken place in the world of work. This has led to increased procrastination in several ways:

- **Overload.** Downsizing and layoffs mean that the people who remain in an organization end up carrying a workload that was intended for two or three people, or even more in extreme cases. The result is employees who become less productive because they're overwhelmed.

- **Change.** Change of management, change of mission and philosophy, change of rules and procedures, change of location or territories, and changes in health plans and benefits—all this change makes people confused and overwhelmed. It messes up routines and breaks down organizational systems, making it difficult to know how to get things done or to find the resources needed to accomplish tasks.

- **Insecurity.** Employers can no longer promise a lifetime of secure employment, which can make employees feel less loyal. If you feel less committed to a person or organization, you'll have less incentive to get things done for them.

- **Self-employment.** Given the changes and lack of security in traditional jobs, more people are opting for the entrepreneurial route by starting businesses, freelancing, or consulting, and they are often doing it from home. Self-employment brings major time-management and organizational challenges. Plus, the success or failure of the business is riding on your shoulders. These external and internal pressures are prime breeding ground for procrastination.

MATTER OF FACT

In the last several years, a whole new genre of career and business books has cropped up to explain what's going on in the workplace and how the changes affect individuals' careers. Some of the best of these books are *Boundaryless Careers: A New Employment Principle for a New Organizational Era* by Michael B. Arthur and *The Opt-Out Revolt: Why People Are Leaving Companies to Create Kaleidoscope Careers* by Lisa Mainiero and Sherry Sullivan.

How Life at Home Leads to Procrastination

Not many households these days have a June Cleaver at home full time doing the cooking, cleaning, and organizing. What you're more likely to find is a dual-income couple trying to juggle the demands of jobs with household chores and children. Or you find single people, either with or without children, working long hours and relying on take-out food and lots of luck in keeping their households functioning.

What ends up happening is that no one's ruling the roost. Most adults in the household are too tired or distracted to plan the meals, cook, clean, and get the bills paid on time. Plus, the old gender stereotypes of who should do which chores are long gone in many households, so no one feels an intrinsic sense of obligation to take out the trash, do the laundry, or put dinner on the table. The result is a lot of people who feel resentful that they have to take care of so many chores on top of their work-related responsibilities and a lot of people who don't have the time or energy to do it all. Those are surefire sparks for an outbreak of procrastination and an invasion of dust bunnies.

> **MATTER OF FACT**
>
> The Procrastination Club of America, founded in 1956, has 12,000 members and—you know what's coming next—millions of would-be members who just haven't gotten around to joining. Don't bother looking for their website. They haven't developed one yet.

To overcome procrastination, you have to know what it is and why you do it. That's what we'll look at in this and the next few chapters.

What Procrastination Is

You might do it all the time or some of the time, but have you ever stopped to analyze just what procrastination is? Procrastination is the act of putting off something until later by not starting it, starting at the last minute, or starting but not finishing. It comes from the Latin words *pro* and *crastinus*, which can be translated as "in favor of tomorrow."

If you're a procrastinator, you probably make vague promises to yourself or others, saying, "I'll do it later." You don't have any idea when later might be; you just know it's not now.

Procrastination often happens with tasks that you expect are going to be difficult, such as quitting smoking. It also happens with projects that seem overwhelming or that you don't know how to begin, such as clearing out clutter that's been building up for years. Or you might put off doing something because it's boring, opting instead to spend your time on more fun or challenging pursuits.

On the other hand, you might be the type who is pretty good about getting things started but runs out of steam midway through and doesn't finish. This kind of procrastination happens frequently with projects that involve many steps and have to be carried out over a long period of time, such as writing reports or reaching self-improvement goals such as getting fit or learning something new. You start out with the best of intentions, but you give up or get distracted before reaching your goals.

> **YOU'RE NOT ALONE**
>
> After all is said and done, more is said than done.
>
> —Anonymous

Things We Procrastinate About

Procrastination can rear its ugly head in any area of your life. Some people are efficient and productive at work but never get anything accomplished on the home front. Others vacuum, floss, and exercise regularly, but procrastinate so often at work that they put their professional future in jeopardy.

For some, it's not a question of whether the task is related to home or work but whether it's big or small, critical or unimportant. There are those who dust regularly, complete routine paperwork at the office, promptly reply to invitations, and wash the car, but never get around to making major life decisions or reaching long-term goals. Others are out saving the world and accomplishing great things, but they put off picking up the dry cleaning or getting their teeth cleaned.

The things we put off or don't finish usually fall into six main categories:

- Home
- Work
- Relationships and social life
- Self-improvement
- School
- Biggies such as finances, insurance, estate planning, and safety

The chapters in Part 3 offer tips for overcoming procrastination in these areas.

For the first edition of this book in 1998, I conducted a survey in which more than 300 respondents from across the world completed an emailed survey to tell me about their procrastination problems. The respondents checked off everything that they procrastinate about and made a special note of the three things that are their biggest procrastination problems, their personal Procrastination Hall of Fame.

Now, more than 10 years later, I updated that survey using the social networking sites Facebook and LinkedIn, as well as via email and personal interviews. I expected that technology would be a major new addition to the list of things people put off at home or work.

I thought people might now say that their biggest procrastination problems are answering email, cleaning out their email inboxes, or organizing their computer files. While those *were* cited as problem areas, they were not at the top of most lists. Just about everyone's top three continued to be many of the low-tech things that the respondents in the late 1990s worried about getting done.

With number 1 as the task most often cited, those that made it into the Procrastination Hall of Fame, both more than a decade ago and now, are the following:

1. Household cleaning
2. Getting organized: receipts, bills, photos, memorabilia, and closets
3. Losing weight
4. Exercising
5. Preparing and filing taxes
6. Scheduling appointments: medical, dental, haircuts
7. Writing thank-you notes
8. Preparing a will or other estate planning
9. Home and auto repairs
10. Yard work

Which of these belongs in your own Procrastination Hall of Fame?

QUICKSAND!

If your goals aren't realistic and feasible, you'll never reach them. Goals that aren't doable are just fantasies.

Why We Love to Hate Procrastination

Most of us have a love-hate relationship with procrastination. We hate the way it wrecks our lives, jeopardizing our health, careers, finances, relationships, and more. We hate the way it puts us in a state of constant worry. At the same time, though, we love the way procrastination relieves us of our responsibilities. It's our little escape from the real world. It gives us permission to go see a good movie instead of studying for a test. It lets us stay in bed an extra hour instead of dragging ourselves to the gym before work. Procrastination makes us human.

When Procrastination Is a Good Thing

You might find this hard to believe, but deciding not to take action is often the best action you can take.

You might, for example, need to spread out commitments and tasks to keep your schedule manageable and to be most productive. Sometimes, you just have to say no to something, or say no to an impossible deadline.

QUICKSAND!

It's easy to trick yourself into thinking that you're doing the good kind of procrastinating when in fact you're looking for an easy way out. Make sure you have a truly legitimate reason for putting something off and are not just making excuses or hoping the task will "go away."

You might also delay something because of an anticipated change in circumstances. You say to yourself, "I'm not going to begin this project yet because it's very likely that the new manager who starts next week is not going to want any of the old manager's special projects to be carried out." As long as you would still have time to get it done if the new person did indeed want it, then you've made a wise decision. But if there's little chance that the project would get cancelled and you're just using the management transition as an excuse to procrastinate, then that's the bad kind of procrastination.

Procrastination is a good thing when it's the result of a conscious, calculated strategy to manage your workload or life in general. It's also a good thing when it lets you stop and smell the roses, have some fun, and live in the present moment, as long as doing so won't have negative consequences in the future.

YOU'RE NOT ALONE

I typically don't do things until dire action requires it. I put off calling the plumber until the leak gets really bad, put off calling the exterminator until I see the mouse myself, procrastinate paying parking tickets until I've received my third urgent notice. Sometimes only the urgency of final deadlines or serious retribution motivates me to do things I don't like doing.

—Jill K., writer

The Cost of Procrastination

Unfortunately, procrastination isn't always a good thing. I guess you know that or you wouldn't be reading this book. Maybe you know about the financial costs of procrastination. You know how cheated you feel shopping for exorbitantly priced roses at 5 P.M. on February 14, or having to pay penalties and interest for late bill payments or taxes filed delinquently. You want to kick yourself for having to pay a higher price for a major household item because you missed the big sale, or having to opt for expensive overnight delivery for the gift you ordered online one day before your Aunt Millie's birthday.

YOU'RE NOT ALONE

My worst procrastination problem is that I put off paying bills, even to the point of having services cut off. The stupid thing is that I always have the money in the bank. I just put off writing the check and mailing it out or pushing the button online to send payment. It is embarrassing how poorly I manage this. I can't explain it. It's almost like I'm addicted to being a bum bill payer.

—Chad P., insurance broker

You might also experience costs of procrastination that don't come with dollar signs, although they are likely to cost you money somewhere down the road. Procrastination can take a toll on your career success, health, and happiness.

If you continually miss deadlines at work, you might get fired. If you keep putting off building a professional network and then get laid off in a downsizing even though you were an excellent worker, you will be behind the eight ball as you start your job search.

When you put off dealing with that little lump, bump, ache, or pain, you might face a much bigger medical problem down the road. When you procrastinate about stopping smoking, getting to a healthy weight, or becoming fit, your health will pay the price eventually.

Then there are the health consequences that aren't so obvious—the ones that affect our quality of life. The constant state of worry and turmoil procrastinators often live under, coupled with the disappointment from missed opportunities or unrealized dreams, can wreak havoc on our mental health and, specifically, our level of contentment in life. Procrastination can cause stress, anxiety, low self-esteem, and even depression. At the very least, it makes us feel just plain unhappy.

The Least You Need to Know

- Procrastination is the act of putting off something until a later time, either by not starting a task or not finishing one you've started.

- Procrastination is a habit that can be broken.

- Procrastination is becoming more common as technological, workplace, and societal changes make life more complex and challenging and offer more distractions.

- Procrastination is sometimes a good thing, but only when it enables you to have a harmless break in life for some fun or when it's the result of a calculated action strategy.

- Chronic procrastination can take a toll on your career success, health, and happiness, as well as come with a high monetary cost.

The Environmental Causes of Procrastination

In This Chapter

- Where procrastination comes from
- Obstacles that slow you down
- How clutter is a roadblock to action
- Common distractions to watch out for

You'll probably be relieved to hear that procrastination is not completely your fault. Although there's no denying that what goes on in your head has a lot to do with procrastination, the root of the problem may be in your environment. Most people, at least those who aren't chronic, frequent procrastinators, don't need years on a shrink's couch to overcome procrastination. (The psychological side of procrastination is covered in Chapter 3.) All you might need is a comfortable, uncluttered, organized, and distraction-free environment that makes it easy to get things done.

I Think, Therefore I Do—or Do I?

Getting started on tasks or completing projects you've begun relies on a critical thought-action link. You have the thought, "I need to do X now," and you expect action to follow, but action doesn't always come, does it? Sometimes obstacles get in the way, breaking up the flow of that thought-action sequence.

Here are some common examples of how your environment can be more to blame than your mind when you procrastinate:

- You may not have a major mental block against exercising; you just don't feel like wading through your messy closet to find clean workout clothes, so you never make it to the gym.

- You might not have a genetic predisposition to avoid housework (then again, you might!); you just don't feel like stooping down to fish around under the kitchen sink for all the cleaning supplies. You particularly don't want to reach for the sponge that always gets hidden behind the pipes where water leaks and where who knows what kinds of creepy-crawlers reside. So you put off housework until a later time because there are just too many steps involved to get to the actual cleaning.

- The reason you're not finishing a project at work may not be that you have a fear of failure, fear of success, or any other fancy psychological hang-up. It could simply be that the disarray of papers and files that have accumulated on your desk makes it difficult to keep track of where you are in the project or the information you need to finish.

- You don't necessarily want to put off your income tax preparation until the last minute because of some deep-seated resentment toward the IRS (though that's a likely reason!). Instead, you might have to put it off because your life is overwhelmed with commitments and obligations that occupy every free minute of your waking hours until April 15.

YOU'RE NOT ALONE

I think I was marked for life as a procrastinator when I saw *Gone with the Wind* as a young man and heard Scarlett O'Hara say, "I'll think of it all tomorrow. After all, tomorrow is another day."

—Scott T., retired dentist

When clutter, disorganization, an overload of commitments, or other distractions get in the way, the link between thought and action becomes weak. These obstacles break the momentum that's needed to get an object into motion. (That object is you, lying on the couch, or staring blankly into space at your desk, or in some other state of inertia.) The obstacles give us a chance to pause or make excuses. We say things like, "If I'm going to do C, I'll have to do A and B first, and that's a real hassle, so I'll do C another time." We default to the easiest route—the path of least resistance. Doing nothing, or doing something easier or more pleasurable, is our preferred path in that moment.

Environmental Hazards

The obstacles that cause procrastination come in three easy-to-remember categories:

- People
- Places
- Things

The people are your partners in crime, the fellow procrastinators who convince you that there are about a million other things you'd rather be doing than the task you're supposed to be doing. They're the ones who keep you tending to your farm on Facebook when you should be studying or working.

They may also be people who are not procrastinators themselves and aren't tempting you with distracting activities but instead are dragging you down by nagging you about getting something done or by not giving you the support and resources you need to get things done. The places are your workspaces, the physical setup, lighting, temperature, and general comfort level of the areas in which you try to get things done, whether that's home, office, or elsewhere.

The things are objects like papers, files, electronic overload, household knick-knacks, junk, old clothes, and anything else that crowds your life and qualifies as clutter. Clutter can also come in the form of commitments and obligations that keep you overworked and overloaded.

The remainder of this chapter focuses on how each of these factors can be a roadblock to action. As you read on, think about your daily life, and see if any of these problems rings true for you. Then, in Part 2 and Part 3, you'll find practical solutions for dealing with these roadblocks.

Peer Pressure and Procrastination

My college roommate probably would have graduated Phi Beta Kappa and gone on to a top 10 law school (those were the ambitions she expressed to me when we moved into our dorm room on the first day of freshman year) if I hadn't egged her on to procrastinate just about every time she needed to be studying or writing a paper into the wee hours. On countless occasions, for example, I persuaded her that it was much more important that we drive into downtown Boston from our college in the 'burbs to a restaurant in Chinatown that was open 24 hours a day.

It wasn't that my powers of persuasion were so impressive but that I was, without realizing it, capitalizing on that weak thought-action link. I was presenting my roommate with a diversion, a thought that was more appealing than the one she had just had. The thought of moo shu pork and pot stickers made her mouth water in a way that her microeconomics textbook just couldn't compete with. So all hope of action—at least the kind that leads to straight As—was gone. (For the record, she did go on to a perfectly respectable law school and became an accomplished attorney with impressive firms.)

ACTION TACTIC

Make a list of all the people you come across in your daily life who may be contributing to your procrastination. Think of ways you could stand up to them and keep them from dragging you back into procrastination mode.

Now, many years later, I'm experiencing payback. As I write this chapter, my teenage daughter is in the next room, texting me frequently, even though she knows I am on a deadline and have to focus (and even though her legs work and she could come talk to me in person).

I knew she hit a high point as a procrastination-enabler when she texted me a link to an online store offering an organic, artisan-carved, Himalayan sea salt block that comes with its own stainless-steel grater to add some "Zen fun to your meals." She insisted that I order it for her right away.

I disobeyed her order (teens are so good at giving orders, aren't they?), reminded her that I must focus on writing, and tried to get back to work. But I couldn't get that salt block out of my mind. I started to imagine shaving it over edamame, or a big steamer of kale, or, who are we kidding, over some greasy waffle fries. That led to me going into the kitchen to make some food. Then I saw the day's mail on the counter and thumbed through some catalogs with more nifty stuff to daydream about. Then I saw the TV in the next room and was about to say, *Well, half an hour won't put me too off-track,* when I remembered that I am writing a book on procrastination and that I'd better know how to keep myself from procrastinating. I employed some of my techniques for getting back on track (which you'll learn about in Chapter 8), and sat back down at my desk and worked ... after I ordered the salt.

The Culture of Procrastination

Procrastination is like a contagious disease; if you're around someone who wants to put off things, you may feel more of an urge to do the same yourself. Like any social behavior, procrastination is fueled by the strength-in-numbers phenomenon. You feel less stigmatized by being a procrastinator and are more likely to give yourself permission to put off things when you see other people doing it. Plus, it's sometimes just plain fun to goof off with your friends, family, co-workers, or online pals, and most people find fun hard to resist.

The Power of Discomfort: How Places Lead to Procrastination

Sometimes you aren't getting things done simply because you're uncomfortable. The chair you're sitting in, the temperature, the constricting clothing you're wearing—all of these things can make you less productive.

QUICKSAND!

Don't abuse the discomfort excuse. If you find that you're often saying things like "I can't work until I find the perfect desk chair" or "It's too hot to do laundry," then you might need to stop making excuses, and just do it.

Sometimes people don't get things done because of something as basic as the temperature. Get up and adjust the air conditioning or heat, open a window, step outside for some fresh air—do whatever you need to do to make your work environment more comfortable and to feel refreshed.

Then there is cubicle, sweet cubicle. The design of most offices—if you can call them offices, given that they usually have no walls, doors, or windows—is not at all conducive to productivity. It's a wonder that anything gets accomplished in corporate America given some of the working conditions. Those lovely cubicle dividers covered in oatmeal-colored carpet, the desk chair that's uncomfortable to sit in after about five minutes, the fluorescent lights that make you feel like a lab experiment—they all add up to one lousy setting for getting things done.

Fortunately, the rats-in-a-maze setup that you find in most office buildings is slowly becoming a thing of the past. More and more employers are realizing that comfortable work environments breed creativity, productivity, and high morale. (They don't want you to be too comfortable, though, so don't try to wheel a recliner into the office Monday morning.)

Of course, not everyone works in a corporate environment or even indoors in an office. The same principles apply, though, regardless of the setting. Your physical workspace affects your productivity no matter what type of job or household chore you're trying to do.

Then there's the clothing issue. If you have a job that requires you to wear formal business attire most of the time, do you find yourself more productive on casual Fridays or other occasions when you get to dress down? Folks who work from home know that there's sometimes nothing more satisfying than working in your bathrobe and scruffy slippers or favorite sweatpants and bare feet.

If you work outside of the home, your employer or clients probably won't be too impressed if you show up in pajamas, but you should think of little ways to make your work attire more comfortable. You might be surprised at the difference in your attitude toward work when your feet aren't being pinched and your shoulders aren't constricted in a suit jacket.

How a Cluttered Life Holds You Back

The third in our deadly trilogy of people, places, and things is things—clutter, stuff, obligations. If you look behind closed doors at the daily life of a procrastinator, you're likely to find too much stuff (papers, files, magazines, newspapers, knick-knacks, and the like) as well as too many commitments that eat up time. If that description fits you, you probably find that clutter slows you down and makes you feel less in control of life.

The Leaning Tower of Paper

Is there a phone call you need to return, but you can't find the phone number among all the scraps of paper on your desk, so you've decided to make the call later? Are you supposed to fill out forms online this week to renew an insurance policy, submit a health-care claim, or to take care of some equally important matter but don't know where you put the paper records you need to fill them out, so you miss the deadline? Are you late mailing a wedding present because you can't remember if the groom's last name is Perkle or Pickle and you can't find the invitation in the seven layers of memorabilia and dry cleaner's receipts on your bulletin board?

Having too much paper—yes, the old hard copy kind—or papers that are disorganized, is one of the major causes of procrastination. It's that thought-action link again. You have the desire, or at least the need, to do something, but you get bogged down in all the paper you have to muddle through before you can take action.

You've probably noticed by now that the paperless office or home that was promised to us by trend analysts at the dawn of the personal computer era never fully materialized. Many of us try to scan, shred, or save instead of print as often as possible, but we still end up with too much paper.

YOU'RE NOT ALONE

It is preoccupation with possession, more than anything else, that prevents men from living freely and nobly.

—Bertrand Russell, early twentieth-century British philosopher and mathematician

You might keep papers because they're important for legal or reference purposes or because you're emotionally attached to them. Sometimes there are perfectly legitimate reasons for holding on to certain papers, even just for sentimental reasons, but the key is to keep only those that are truly important or special and to keep them well organized. In Chapter 6, you'll find lots of tips for getting yourself to throw things out and for finding a good place for the papers you do keep. (And I'm not talking about the proverbial safe place that eats paper like some homespun Bermuda Triangle.)

Electronic Clutter

It would take an awful lot of file cabinets to store the amount of information that can fit on a computer's hard drive or in web-based storage. This storage capacity is impressive, but it's also dangerous in that computers can easily become repositories for vast amounts of useless or irrelevant data.

> **ACTION TACTIC**
>
> Open your calendar (yes, *now*) and schedule a block of time on a specific date (probably one to two hours are needed) when you'll go through your hard drive to discard files and programs you don't need and to reorganize your files and folders.

If I were to take a look at your computer desktop right now, what would I find on it? Your 2008 holiday gift list? The letter you wrote to your next-door neighbor 10 years ago complaining about the tree growing into your property? A fact sheet on the migration patterns of Tasmanian marsupials downloaded from the Discovery Channel's website? A folder of unimportant email you saved during the first month you got online many moons ago because you were so taken with this amazing new communication method that you just had to preserve it for posterity?

Computers in homes and offices are among the most overlooked clutter traps. They look innocent enough, sitting there on the desk or as a laptop tucked neatly into a pouch with no telltale signs of the junk hidden within (unlike closets and drawers, which always seem to have something spilling out of them as a reminder of the chaos that lurks within). Like any type of clutter, an excess of electronic files and folders, incoming or saved email, and outdated or underutilized programs or applications slows you down when you're trying to get things done.

There's no denying that in many ways, computers and other electronic gadgets enable us to be more productive than we ever would be without them. But if we let them become clutter traps, they can make us feel dazed and confused and unable to do what matters.

The Collector's Curse

Not all clutter comes in the form of paper or electronic files. Those 30-plus camel figurines that used to be scattered about my house that caused me to put off dusting until the last possible moment probably counted as clutter. I love my camel collection, but I hate the way it makes a fairly easy chore much more difficult than it ought to be, so I have culled it down to a few favorite ones that I leave out. The rest are safely stored away.

What do you have around the house or office that makes your life more difficult? There's nothing wrong with collecting things you like or saving objects that have sentimental or monetary value. I'm not saying you have to live like a monk. But if you've been collecting things that don't have any great meaning for you or any current or future market value, is there any reason to keep them? If you've become a slave to your collections, then it might be time to part company with them. You'll read more about how to do this in Chapter 6.

Commitment Overload

Clutter doesn't have to consist only of tangible objects. It also comes in the form of things you have to do. Your life may be crowded with so many commitments and responsibilities that you can't handle being pulled in that many different directions. When this happens, you may become overwhelmed, shut down, and not do anything. Even ordinarily productive and efficient people procrastinate when there's too much to do.

QUICKSAND!

Having an extraordinary amount of responsibilities and obligations in your personal and professional life is nothing to brag about. Don't make the mistake of judging your or others' self-worth by how much you have to do. Truly accomplished people have balanced lives, not overextended ones.

Many people find that they are more productive when they're busy than when they have nothing to do and no structure to their lives. But when that busyness is taken too far and becomes an overload of responsibilities, the opposite happens. People become overwhelmed and unable to function. Every time they think of working on one project, their minds start spinning with all the other things they have to do. The energy they expend worrying about those other commitments drains the energy they need for the task at hand. In Chapter 5, you'll learn ways to turn down commitment requests as well as ways to get out of or minimize obligations you've already committed to.

So Is It Really Not My Fault?

Now that you see how many obstacles in your life might be fueling procrastination, you might be tempted to close this book here and say, "I don't need to know any more. I now know that I procrastinate because my office is always too hot." I'm sorry to tell you that it's not that simple. Factors such as clutter, commitments, other people, and distractions may be the catalyst for your procrastination, but they don't tell the whole story. It's still up to you and all those thoughts and feelings in your head to determine how you react to your environment. You can choose to give in to the obstacles and procrastinate, or you can choose to get things done. The next chapter will look at how that process works.

The Least You Need to Know

- Procrastination results from a combination of psychological and environmental factors.
- You might procrastinate because people around you encourage and enable the procrastination.
- Procrastination can result from working in a physically uncomfortable space.
- An excess of paper, electronic stuff, and possessions, as well as an overload of commitments, can lead to procrastination.
- You have control over how you react to your environment, and you don't have to give in to procrastination.

The Internal Causes of Procrastination

In This Chapter

* How thoughts and feelings lead to procrastination
* Where habits come from
* How to know whether fear is holding you back
* When being perfect gets in the way
* When procrastination signals a more serious problem

Procrastination may not be completely your fault, as Chapter 2 explains. Those external factors can prevent you from starting or finishing a task or reaching goals. But no matter who or what is conspiring against you as you try to take action, it's still you and only you who is ultimately responsible for the action you take—or don't take. To beat procrastination, you have to own up to the fact that what goes on in your head has something to do with the problem.

Understanding the Psychology of Action

All actions result from thoughts and feelings. If those thoughts and feelings are negative, irrational, or unrealistic, then the behavior they spark may turn out to be procrastinating behavior. If they're neutral or positive, then the behavior that results from them is more likely to be productive and appropriate.

Let's look at how thoughts and feelings can influence actions, first with an irrational thought and negative emotion reacting to the routine need to fold and put away clean laundry:

> **Irrational thought:** This pile of laundry is such a mess, I'll never get it done. This is a huge job.

> **Negative emotional reaction:** Why can't I make more money so I can afford to have a housekeeper who does this for me? I just can't ever seem to get ahead in life.

YOU'RE NOT ALONE

When I try to make myself do something I don't want to do, it's as if I'm in that movie *Invasion of the Body Snatchers*. I know I have ultimate control over what I think and feel, but sometimes I feel like someone else is in my head telling me I don't have to do something. I feel like I'm my own worst enemy.

—Adrienne G., homemaker and mother

Now take a look at how a more rational and positive thought process and emotional reaction can lead to more productive behavior in the same situation:

> **Rational thought:** Wow. That's one big pile of laundry. But I've done it before and I know I can do it again. These simple tasks never turn out to be as painful as they seem like they're going to be.

> **Positive emotional reaction:** Wouldn't it be nice to have somebody do this for me? But I can't afford that right now, and that's okay. I feel good about myself in other areas of my life.

Such head games might seem like an exaggeration when it comes to a task as mundane as laundry. But if you pause for a moment and think about what you might be saying to yourself or feeling when faced with any task you often put off, I bet you'll realize you're playing some of the same games. And now you can see how easy it is to substitute positive thoughts and feelings for the negative ones. It's those positive ones that will spur you into action.

How Thinking Too Much Leads to Procrastination

Sometimes procrastinating behavior results from thinking too much. You worry about the outcome of an endeavor you're about to undertake or stew over how far behind you are on an assignment for school. Instead of following the advice of Nike to "just do it," you work yourself into a frenzy by thinking about what's wrong with your situation or what could go wrong. You end up making the task much more difficult or overwhelming than it needs to be and start feeling down on yourself for slacking off. Those feelings can lead to a negative self-concept or low self-esteem, which in turn fuel further procrastination.

MATTER OF FACT

The thought-feeling-action link described here is based on the work of psychologist Albert Ellis, who pioneered a very practical and well-respected type of cognitive psychotherapy called rational emotive behavior therapy (REBT). What I cover in this chapter is just the tip of the iceberg, so if you want a more in-depth look at REBT, go to the site of the Albert Ellis Institute at www.rebt.org.

How Not Thinking Enough Leads to Procrastination

You might also procrastinate because you don't think enough. You may act impulsively without thinking through what you are doing. Suppose that every night after dinner you say to yourself, "I ought to clean up the kitchen now rather than leaving everything sitting here until morning." Then, without thinking about the negative consequences of putting off that task (such as the fact that the pots and pans will have all sorts of crud stuck to them by morning), you go off to do something else and ignore the dishes and leftover food sitting out.

> **ACTION TACTIC**
>
> The next time you're about to put off something that you habitually procrastinate over, listen to the thoughts running through your head. Do you hear any self-talk like "I'll do it later" or "I don't have to do this now"? If so, think about how much power those simple little statements have been having over your behavior.

Somewhere between that first thought and the action of leaving the kitchen was a fleeting thought that said, "I'll do it later." You block from your mind all thoughts of the messy kitchen and go on to more pleasant thoughts and activities.

If you don't stop and zero in on that "I'll do it later" thought, and if you don't consciously think through the consequences of your decision to put off the cleaning, then you'll stay in the same old pattern of acting on impulse. Habits develop in this way, and procrastination is one of the worst habits of all. In Chapter 8, you'll learn about the stop, look, and listen solution, which helps you focus on and fix the faulty thoughts and feelings that are causing you to act on impulse.

What's Causing Your Procrastination?

The thoughts and feelings swirling around in your head can lead to procrastination in several ways. Those ways fall into 10 main categories:

1. **Fear:** Fear of failure, success, or how you'll be judged

2. **Perfectionism:** Making tasks more difficult and the anticipated outcomes more critical than they need to be

3. **Being overwhelmed:** Finding a task so difficult or cumbersome that you don't know where or how to begin or end it

4. **Feeling frustrated:** Having a low tolerance for the ambiguity or delayed gratification that comes with some projects

5. **Adrenaline rush addiction:** Relying on the thrill that comes from getting something done at the last minute

6. **Negativity toward the task:** Disliking or being uninterested in the task itself

7. **Rebellion:** Having negative feelings toward the person who assigned a task or who will benefit from it and resenting that you have to do it

8. **Unrealistic view of time:** Having a faulty sense of time and how much you can get done within it

9. **Psychological issues:** Disorders such as clinical depression or attention deficit disorder, among others, make it difficult to get things done

10. **Physical problem:** Having a physical ailment that drains your energy and makes you less likely to get things done

You probably procrastinate for different reasons at different times, so more than one of those 10 causes is likely to ring a bell. To overcome your procrastination and implement the strategies suggested in Parts 2 and 3 of this book, you must first understand the source of your problem. As you read the rest of this chapter, try to relate each cause to your situation and focus on the ones that are relevant for you.

Fears That Hold You Back

Fear is a handy defense mechanism. Being fearful keeps us from trying new things, taking risks, or accepting challenges. Fear defends and protects us because it keeps us from doing the things that we could fail at or be harshly judged because of. What this means for procrastinators is that fear keeps us from starting or finishing projects that could have possible negative outcomes or consequences.

The fears that relate to procrastination include the following:

- Fear of failure

- Fear of being judged

- Fear of success

The following sections describe how each of these fears could be holding you back.

ACTION TACTIC

To make fear of failure less of a problem, try to remember a time when you did fail at something but found that the people you care about were supportive and didn't think any less of you.

Fear of Failure

If you don't enter the race, you can't lose. By not entering, you miss out on the satisfaction and rewards that might come from winning, but at least you won't have to face the disappointment of losing or lose face in front of others.

Failure is something most people want to avoid. It hurts emotionally by making you feel disappointed, sad, and rejected. It might embarrass or even humiliate you if the failure is at all public. It also can damage your self-esteem and self-confidence. From a practical standpoint, failure can have dire consequences. You might not earn an academic degree, get the job you want, or be rewarded with more money, the corner office, or whatever it is that you want or need. If you are avoiding "entering the race" because you're afraid you won't win, fear of failure may be causing your procrastination.

Fear of Being Judged

The fear of being judged is related to the idea of fearing failure but has more to do with the quality of your work or your performance. You may have experienced fear of being judged during your years as a student. Whether your school days are in the distant past or part of your present, the fear of getting a bad grade is probably etched in your mind. If you received a lousy grade from time to time (or often), it was always easier to deal with the situation when you could say, "But I didn't study at all," or "I didn't start writing the paper until the night before." Telling others (and yourself) that you made no effort or didn't give it your all let everyone know that the grade didn't reflect your ability, so you were off the hook.

Not everything we do in life gets a grade from A to F, but most things we do are judged in some way. Whether it's a fussy guest giving your cleaning ability the white glove test or co-workers and bosses judging your presentation skills at a staff meeting, someone is always scrutinizing the things you do. If you are particularly sensitive to or concerned about how you're going to be judged on a certain task, then you may be more likely to delay starting it or finishing it.

YOU'RE NOT ALONE

Fear can be headier than whiskey, once man has acquired a taste for it.

—Donald Downes, twentieth-century American novelist

Fear of Success

I first heard the term fear of success way back in the late 1970s when there was lots of talk about superwomen, women who were finding success in their careers while meeting the demands of family life. Fear of success was sometimes given as an excuse for why some women were not reaching even higher levels in the professional world.

My first reaction was, "How bogus! Why would anyone be afraid of success, especially someone who has made a point of positioning herself or himself on the road to success? Who wouldn't want to be accomplished?" About 50 psychology classes and a lot of life experience later, I came to realize that the term does make sense. It's not that some people don't want to succeed. They are simply afraid of how their lives may change if they do achieve success.

If we succeed once, we're expected to do it again, or to be even more successful the next time. Sometimes it seems easier not to try at all than to set ourselves on a track where people will have increasingly high expectations for us—or that we'll have for ourselves. Having a fear of success doesn't mean that you wouldn't want to be successful. It just means that you aren't comfortable with what would be expected of you or how your identity might change if you did achieve success.

When Perfection Is Part of the Problem

Striving for excellence is a good thing. Striving to be perfect is not. What's the difference? Perfectionists are extreme and obsessive in their thinking. They become preoccupied with being perfect and are often controlling in their efforts to reach perfection. There's nothing wrong with wanting to give 100 percent effort to a project or having high standards for how you carry it out. There is something wrong with thinking that everything you do must be done flawlessly.

People who are not perfectionists and who merely have high standards for their behavior and their work are more realistic and flexible. They want to do well, but they understand that perfectionism is an impossible goal and that being slightly less than perfect is still acceptable.

Perfectionism is one of the most common causes of procrastination. If you are determined to have everything you do turn out flawlessly, then you probably make every task more difficult than it needs to be. To a perfectionist, even the smallest task becomes a major ordeal, and the truly big projects seem insurmountable. As perfectionists embark on new projects, they remember how much effort went into a similar one in the past and feel tired and overwhelmed before even beginning the task at hand. Perfectionists try to maintain such impossibly high standards that they end up burning themselves out.

YOU'RE NOT ALONE

Every time I find that I'm getting in my own way, the advice of my first boss [Ronald Mansbridge, former Director of Cambridge University Press] rings in my ears. He told me, "Don't let the perfect stand in the way of the good."

—Sally Dougan, Bert Davis Executive Search

For example, I am a perfectionist who has always struggled not to be one. As I was writing this section on perfectionism, I was thinking, "I have to write the most intelligent, original, innovative, and clinically accurate description of perfectionism that's ever been written.

A lot of people have written about perfectionism, and I want my account of it to be different and better." (Okay, so maybe I'm competitive, not a perfectionist.)

So what did I do after having that thought and writing the first three sentences of the section? I went to the kitchen for another glass of water. I checked my phone to see if I'd missed any calls or texts. I went on Facebook to see if anyone had posted anything interesting since the last time I checked 10 minutes before. In other words, I procrastinated.

What got me back to writing? Besides the pressure of looming deadlines in my contract (nothing like a legal document to get a person motivated!), I got back to writing by telling myself, "It doesn't have to be perfect, it just has to be very good, and, most important, it has to get done."

How Mind Games Slow Us Down

The same faulty thoughts and feelings that lead to perfectionism can also cause you to procrastinate for other reasons. You might give in to feelings of being overwhelmed, frustrated, or bored by a task and not attempt to do it or give up before completing it. You might also react by rebelling against the people or institutions that expect you to get something done. Or you might misjudge how long it will take to complete a task or project and wait until the last minute to start it.

All of this cognitive and emotional turmoil means that you're letting your responsibilities and commitments get the best of you.

Feeling Overwhelmed

Some people let themselves get overwhelmed by the size, scope, or nature of a project. If you find a task you're facing to be difficult or overly challenging, you might not even attempt it or may give up too quickly rather than seeking the information and support that would help you complete it. Feeling overwhelmed also happens when a project involves many steps. You get in the middle of the project and lose sight of what to do next, particularly if your surroundings are cluttered and disorganized.

ACTION TACTIC

If you don't know how to begin a project because you weren't given adequate instructions, ask for more guidance. You'll look less stupid asking for clarification at the beginning than you will down the road when you haven't finished it or have made mistakes.

This Is So Frustrating!

Feeling frustrated is a lot like feeling overwhelmed. Frustration is often a problem when a project is underway and is either not going well or seems never-ending. Some projects require that you stay patient and wait for delayed gratification. If you're the sort of person who needs to see immediate results, then you might end up giving up and saying you'll try again another time. This outcome is especially common with long-term endeavors such as weight loss. If you've tried to lose weight, how many times have you given up because you weren't losing quickly enough to keep yourself motivated to stick with the plan?

The Adrenaline Rush

Some procrastinators are addicted to the rush of adrenaline that comes from completing a task at the last minute. They get a sort of natural high from the thrill of pulling out all the stops and beating incredible odds to meet a deadline. (Of course, that high might also be from the huge amounts of caffeine procrastinators usually consume in order to stay awake and alert to get things finished!)

If you're the type who is always racing against the clock, think about why that might be. Some people who love the last-minute adrenaline rush simply crave some excitement in their lives. They put off things until the last minute because their work or their lives are so dull that they need to introduce a little excitement. Others do so because they believe they do their best work that way. (I used to be one of those, and sometimes still am.) Maybe they do good work, but might their results be even better if they gave themselves a little more time?

Others addicted to adrenaline need it to boost their self-esteem. If they create a crisis by waiting until the last minute to do something, and then solve the crisis by getting that thing done, they end up looking like heroes who have saved the day in their own minds and to others who witness their accomplishment.

I'm So Bored

You might put off doing something because it doesn't interest you. How you feel about a task is directly linked to how likely you are to get it started or finished. You may know the feeling of starting on a project with a gung-ho attitude only to find that you get so bored with it midway through that you abandon it and never finish. That may be why there are so many unfinished home do-it-yourself projects and unused filing systems around the world.

 QUICKSAND!

You might enjoy the adrenaline rush that comes from doing things at the last minute and see no harm in it as long as you ultimately get your work done; but think how your procrastination affects the people around you. It may be unfair to force friends, family, or co-workers to live on the edge with you.

You Want Me to Do What?!

Procrastination is a powerful tool for rebellion. If you hate your boss, it can feel awfully good to show how insignificant her little pet project is by not getting around to doing it. If your husband nags you to wash your car more often and you don't understand why the matter should concern him, you show your power by driving around in a car that always looks like you just came back from off-roading.

When other people try to control the way we do our work or carry out our lives, we often rebel by not doing what they want us to do. By putting off or never getting around to completing chores or projects they think are important, we exert some control over our lives and keep others from taking over. A little rebellion is necessary for our sanity and independence, but when carried too far, it can put our jobs, businesses, and relationships in jeopardy.

When a More Serious Issue Might Be to Blame

For most people, procrastination is a bad habit they've picked up and can't seem to shake because of the powerful psychological hold that habits can have. But sometimes procrastination signals a more serious mental health issue. The following disorders are often associated with procrastination:

- Attention deficit disorder (ADD) or attention deficit hyperactivity disorder (ADHD)

- Obsessive-compulsive disorder (OCD)

- Anxiety

- Depression

I'm not saying that procrastination and psychological disorders always go hand in hand, but if you find that your procrastination is chronic and extreme and is having a seriously negative impact on your life, then one of these issues could possibly be the culprit. Diagnosing any of these disorders is beyond the scope of this book; you'd have to meet with a professional counselor, psychologist, or psychiatrist in order to get a complete, accurate diagnosis.

QUICKSAND!

Only a qualified, licensed mental health professional can accurately diagnose a psychological disorder. Don't try to diagnose or treat yourself, and don't be afraid or embarrassed to seek help.

Medical Reasons for Procrastination

The physical symptoms you have when procrastinating may feel a lot like the ones you get with the flu or jet lag. You lack energy, feel sluggish, and walk around (or lie around) in a kind of daze.

Sometimes, the similarity is more than a coincidence. Your behavior (delaying starting something or running out of steam after starting) may be rooted in a physical problem rather than a psychological one.

Although you should, of course, see a physician for regular checkups, you may particularly want to pay attention to your physical health if you're experiencing serious problems with procrastination. That way, you'll know if you can rule out something like a fatigue syndrome or other illness and can get on with tackling the environmental or psychological causes of your procrastination.

You're Not a Bad Person

If you're fed up with procrastinating, then you're probably fed up with yourself, too. You might feel lazy, undisciplined, irresponsible, and doomed to a life of missed opportunities. Although it certainly doesn't hurt to be a little tough on yourself to help get you moving, don't take the self-criticism too far, or you'll only make matters worse.

Procrastination is not a character flaw you were born with. It's a behavioral problem you've developed, a habit you've learned. (One exception to this rule is when procrastinating results from something like attention deficit disorder, obsessive-compulsive disorder, a learning disability, clinical depression, or other difficulties you might have been born with or developed. These problems are explained in Chapter 4.)

ACTION TACTIC

If you're feeling down on yourself for procrastinating too much, take a few moments to think about times in the past when you accomplished something, or things you accomplish now. Even if you're feeling lousy about yourself, realizing how much you have done and do on a regular basis should provide some encouragement.

Don't Worry, There Is Hope

Procrastination can feel like an addiction. You may have the sensation of being out of control and powerless to do anything about it. You feel as though some force within is controlling your actions. You can't figure out where that force comes from or how to curb it. Just as is sometimes the case with addictions to alcohol, drugs, gambling, shopping, or food, procrastinating behavior is often the result of giving in to impulses, having a negative self-concept, or being in an environment that enables the habit. Unlike some other addictions, however, procrastination is not a disease. It is simply a habit, a habit you can have power over.

The point of this chapter was to introduce you to some of the causes of procrastination that might result from thoughts and feelings you have when facing a task. If you think that any of these issues are responsible for some or all of your own procrastination, and if they seem like insurmountable problems, don't despair. Parts 2 and 3 of this book are devoted to showing how you can cross these hurdles with a minimum of pain and suffering.

The Least You Need to Know

- Procrastination often results from irrational or negative thoughts and feelings that lead to unproductive behavior.
- Some people procrastinate because they fear how they'll be judged, or they fear success or failure.
- Problems like perfectionism or feeling overwhelmed or frustrated can keep you from starting or completing tasks.
- Some procrastinators are addicted to the adrenaline rush that comes from doing things at the last minute.
- It's sometimes a good idea to consult a mental health professional or physician to make sure your procrastination is not related to a mental or physical condition.

Why You've Failed in the Past

In This Chapter

- What keeps you from getting yourself moving
- Why change is such a chore
- How to calculate your chances of success
- Why having a support team is key

You should now have a handle on what procrastination is and why it happens. This can mean only one thing: the time to take action is near. Soon, you'll have to venture into those bulging closets and drawers, return to that half-written novel, take the car in for servicing, face up to a career or relationship that's going nowhere, or do whatever it is you need to do to stop putting your life on hold.

If you're getting cold feet at this point, that might be because you're remembering all the times in the past when you tried to turn over a new leaf and nothing happened. Maybe the new you lasted only a day, a week, or even a month, before you were back to your old ways. A backlog of projects piled up, your to-do list gathered dust, your home or office became cluttered again, and life started to feel out of control once more. It doesn't have to be that way this time. In this chapter, you'll learn why your past efforts to overcome procrastination have failed and what you're going to do to make it work this time.

QUICKSAND!

Even if you aren't having any doubts about your ability to break the procrastination habit, don't assume you can skip this chapter. The confidence and motivation you feel now might wane in a few days or weeks. That's not pessimism; it's reality.

Why Your Past Efforts Have Failed

If you've struck out a few times when you've tried to stop procrastinating and make positive behavioral changes in life, your failure was probably caused by one or more of the following factors:

- **You lacked commitment.** You may have thought you wanted to stop procrastinating, but you hadn't fully committed to the idea. Perhaps you were merely trying to do what others wanted you to do, but you didn't care all that much about making changes in your life. Or maybe you did want to change but weren't willing to make sacrifices.

- **You tried to do too much, too soon.** Maybe you tried to solve everything at once. You took stock of all the current crises, looming deadlines, and backburner projects you'd been putting off and decided to tackle them simultaneously. That's a recipe for disaster.

- **You didn't get instant gratification.** If you expected to see dramatic changes in your behavior and your life simply because you said the magic words, "I'm not going to procrastinate anymore," you might have been disappointed when instant gratification didn't come. Old habits die hard, and change takes time.

QUICKSAND!

Some people think they're committed to kicking the procrastination habit for good, but in reality they just want a quick fix. In the back of their minds, they expect to go back to their old ways as soon as some immediate problems or urgent matters are dealt with. If you don't make a serious commitment, it'll be just a matter of time before you backslide.

- **You didn't prioritize.** Perhaps you dove right in and started trying to finish things without first determining what was most important to you and to the significant people around you. You have to believe in what you're doing in order to get it done.

- **You weren't angry enough.** Sometimes you have to get to the point of saying, "I'm mad as hell and I'm not going to take it anymore," before you can get yourself moving. At first, the anger is often directed at someone else, such as the person who gets ahead of you in life while you're busy procrastinating or maybe the person who monopolizes your time and keeps you from getting things done. But eventually, you have to realize that the blame lies primarily with yourself and become so exasperated that you finally decide to do something about the problem.

- **You weren't scared enough.** As with anger, fear of damaging consequences plays a big part in attempts to become an ex-procrastinator. You may have to realize how unpleasant the potential consequences of procrastination are before you can fully commit to giving up the more pleasurable alternative behaviors you engage in while putting off the less fun stuff.

- **You lacked support.** It's difficult to go it alone when trying to make major, or even minor, changes in life. If you tried to turn over a new leaf in the past and didn't have a team of key people helping you (friends, family, co-workers, or experts of some sort), you probably didn't manage to keep that leaf turned over for very long.

- **You lacked information.** To accomplish something, you have to know how to do it. Depending on the nature of the task or project, you may need information, guidance, skills, and resources. If a lack of know-how or resources has held you back in the past, think about why. Were you afraid to ask for help? Did you not know where to turn for guidance?

- **Your timing was off.** Even though it's not a good idea to wait for the proverbial perfect time to do something, there is such a thing as choosing the wrong time to get over your procrastination. Never try to make behavioral changes when your life is overloaded with commitments and pressing deadlines or when major life-changing events are taking place.

ACTION TACTIC

Think of one behavioral change you've made or habit you've broken in the past. Why did it work that time? Pinpointing the root of your success helps you repeat the success.

- **You weren't balanced.** If your life doesn't have a healthy balance of work and play, or action and relaxation, you'll burn out. Just what that balance should be is different for each person, but whatever it is, you have to pay attention to it. You have to nurture the part of you that wants to goof off as much as you nudge the part of you that has to be, and wants to be, productive.

- **You had an identity crisis.** Identity crises don't only happen at key age-related stages in life, such as adolescence, midlife, or retirement. They can pop up any time you try to change your behavior. Habits, both good and bad, become such second nature that they become a big part of your identity. When you try to change those habits, you also have to change the way you see yourself and the way you want others to see you. This process can be unsettling and may cause you to abandon your efforts to change.

- **You took the easy way out.** No matter what obstacles are standing in your way and no matter how difficult change is, there comes a time when you have to be tough on yourself and stop making excuses, whining, and looking for the perfect time or magic shortcut. This time you're not going to let yourself give up too easily.

YOU'RE NOT ALONE

Every new adjustment is a crisis in self-esteem.

—Eric Hoffer, twentieth-century American writer and social commentator

These reasons for abandoning your effort to break the procrastination habit are normal reactions to the challenges that the change process brings. Any way you cut it, making behavioral changes is difficult.

Why Change Is So Darn Hard

If it were easy to break bad habits and change problem behavior, the world would be a very different place. You'd see lots of slim, physically fit people walking around, the tobacco industry would crumble, executive coaches wouldn't have any clients, and bill collectors would have no one to call. But the world doesn't look like that, because bad habits, especially procrastination, are as hard to get rid of as telemarketers at dinnertime. Change is difficult because …

- It takes time.

- It takes effort.

- It's hard to do alone.

- It leads you into unfamiliar territory.

ACTION TACTIC

Make a list of at least five positive changes you've made in your life in the past. They might be changes in your appearance, health, financial status, career, social life, home, or anything at all. It doesn't matter whether the changes lasted. The important thing is that you made them. Seeing the list can get you motivated to make changes again.

One of the best ways to bring about change in your life is to understand the process of change itself. If you realize that changes take time and effort, and you anticipate that they'll be a little unsettling and isolating, then you have realistic expectations.

Understanding the Seven Stages of Change

When you're trying to overcome procrastination, you'll probably find yourself going through seven typical stages of the change process:

1. Acknowledge the need to change your behavior. Wake up to the fact that procrastination is not a cute personality quirk; it's a dangerous habit that threatens your health, wealth, and happiness, as well as that of people around you.

2. Declare to yourself and to others that you're ready to change. Make it official. Some people refrain from telling anyone that they're going to try to break a habit for fear of embarrassment if they don't succeed. But telling other people about your plans makes you accountable for your behavior and reinforces your commitment.

3. Mentally prepare yourself to commit to making a change. While you work on breaking the habit, think through how your life will be different when you change it and what you'll think and feel. Brace yourself for at least a little inconvenience and emotional pain.

4. Figure out how to change. Don't expect yourself to have an innate sense of how to make a behavioral change. Change is an acquired skill, not something you necessarily have an intuitive knack for. Seek professional help if you need to.

5. Develop and implement a change strategy. Follow a step-by-step process that makes sense for the type of change you need to make. Do some research, network, consult experts—whatever it takes to develop a plan that will work. Of course, because the change you're focusing on now is to stop procrastinating, this book can serve as your resource for a strategy.

6. Get frustrated and accept setbacks. If the change process were plotted on a graph, it would look like those jagged lines with peaks and valleys we see on graphs of things such as

interest rates or the level of unemployment in America. For every two forward steps you take, there's inevitably going to be a backward step. If you are aware of this from the outset, you'll be less likely to give up when you become frustrated.

7. Work through the frustration and past the setbacks until a new behavior gradually replaces the old habits. As you keep plugging away through the change process, you will wake up one day and realize that your new behavior has started to feel like a habit. You will have replaced the do-it-later habit with the do-it-now habit.

After you've made your way through these stages, you'll need to cycle back through them periodically to maintain your new way of doing things. This maintenance process is addressed in Chapter 14.

How Likely Are You to Change?

So now that you know what change is like, what are the chances that you're going to be able to overcome procrastination? Take the following quiz to find out. Circle True (T), False (F), or Not Sure (NS) to indicate how you feel about each statement. Be honest!

T	F	NS	I am completely fed up with my procrastination.
T	F	NS	I fear that severe negative consequences are just around the corner (or already here) if I keep putting things off.
T	F	NS	I can be patient with the change process and comfortable with the fact that it might take a long time to break my bad habits.
T	F	NS	I am okay with the idea that I might have to give up some leisure and fun time for a while in order to get more critical things done.
T	F	NS	I have the courage to admit to other key people in my life that procrastination is a big problem for me.

continues

continued

T	F	NS	I am willing to put myself on more of a daily schedule and routine.
T	F	NS	I am willing to ask others for help and to delegate some responsibilities.
T	F	NS	I am aware that much of the paper and possessions in my home and/or office will have to be thrown out or given away, and I am okay with that. (Or if already clutter free, I can commit to keeping it that way.)
T	F	NS	I can learn to say no to commitments and obligations.
T	F	NS	I can honestly say that I know I deserve to be happy and successful, in whichever way I choose to define those concepts.

The scoring for this quiz is simple: you either pass or fail; there's no middle ground. If you answered False or Not Sure to even one of these statements, you need to rethink your commitment to overcoming procrastination. It's normal and natural to be unsure about or unable to agree with a few of these statements. But if you do, be aware that your likelihood of success goes down a notch or two. In order to make significant changes in your behavior, you need to get to the point where you can agree with all 10 statements.

YOU'RE NOT ALONE

I use not only all the brains I have, but all I can borrow.

—Woodrow Wilson, twenty-eighth president of the United States

Creating an Amateur Support Team

Of all the tactics you'll use to overcome procrastination, having a support team is one of the most important. A support team isn't a team in the literal sense. You don't need to type up a roster and print up T-shirts with team members' names on the back and some sort of Procrastination Busters logo on the front. (Although, if it makes you happy to do so, by all means, knock yourself out.) Your amateur support team is an inner circle of people to turn to for advice, strategy, resources, encouragement, and emotional support.

QUICKSAND!

Be careful when you seek help from people who are extremely efficient, productive, and successful. If they're too self-righteous about their way of doing things, they might make you feel inferior. Don't include anyone in your inner circle who could damage your self-esteem.

The people you turn to for emotional support when the going gets tough or for advice and strategies when you run out of ideas may include family, friends, work colleagues, teachers or professors, and your virtual networks and online communities.

Out of these categories, exactly who you need on your team depends on the nature of the things you procrastinate about and the type of support you respond to best. Some people, for example, are more comfortable talking to friends about their problems than they are talking to their families. Others may not want to share their problems even with close friends and family and prefer to seek the confidential support that comes from a professional such as a psychotherapist.

Getting Support from the Pros

Maybe your situation is too serious for an amateur pep talk to make a difference. It might be time to call in the big guns—the experts who can coach and counsel you through changing your behavior, getting organized, or reaching your goals. Your choices for an objective, expert ear fall into four basic categories:

- Mental health professionals
- Career development professionals
- Personal or life coaches
- Professional organizers

Mental Health Professionals

If you are suffering from chronic or severe procrastination that is causing distress to you or the people around you, then it might be time to consult with a qualified mental health professional for some psychotherapy to work through the issues that are holding you back. But people who need professional help for a procrastination problem often put off getting that help because they don't know how to find the right person.

The key to sorting out the choices is to have a basic understanding of what the various educational degrees, licenses, and titles mean.

MATTER OF FACT

Working one on one with a mental health professional, career counselor, coach, or organizer in private practice is not the only way to get expert advice. You can save time and money in a group counseling or seminar setting and have the added benefit of camaraderie and networking opportunities To find support groups or seminars, contact universities (especially the adult education or continuing education division), professional associations for the field or industry in which you work, places of worship, hospitals or health clinics, your employer's employee assistance program, and social service agencies or community centers.

Mental health professionals might be designated by any of the following:

- **Psychiatrist.** This is a medical doctor with MD after his or her name. Psychiatrists often focus more on diagnosis of clinical issues and treatment with medication or other medical approaches, rather than counseling and therapy, though some will provide talk therapy.

- **Psychologist.** Degrees include PhD and PsyD, with specializations including counseling psychology, clinical psychology, or educational psychology.

- **Counselor.** Degrees include MA, MS, MSW, CSW, MDiv, and more. Some have educational backgrounds in psychological counseling, pastoral counseling, social work, or nursing, and many have a professional counseling licensure such as LPC for Licensed Professional Counselor.

In the "Questions to Ask When Seeking Professional Help" section later in this chapter, you'll find guidance for how to determine which mental health professional is right for you.

Career Development Professionals

If your tooth aches, you go to a dentist. If your eyesight needs to be checked, you see an optometrist or ophthalmologist. Rarely would you try to fix these problems yourself. So why suffer through job or career problems without the help of a professional trained in those matters?

People with expertise in career management and job hunting can help you choose a career direction, make a career change, find a job, get a promotion or raise, or improve your on-the-job performance and satisfaction. If you've been putting off doing something about your career, then a visit to a career development professional may be what you need to get moving.

As with psychotherapy, career advice is dispensed by a dizzying array of professionals and so-called professionals. Here are some of the titles you're likely to come across:

- Career counselor
- Career consultant
- Career management consultant
- Career coach
- Career strategist
- Career advisor
- Job search coach
- Employment consultant
- Executive coach

Those who call themselves career counselors must have a Master's degree or higher in psychology, counseling, or social work. Beyond that, their credentials and experience vary widely, because career counseling is a largely unregulated field. Some states require licenses, and some career counselors have obtained optional credentials such as the National Certified Career Counselor designation.

Career development professionals who do not have a counseling or psychology degree often have backgrounds in business and call themselves career consultants or coaches. They tend to focus more on helping clients with strategies for a career change or job-hunting processes, as well as on-the-job performance issues, than with the more psychological issues that come up when making career choices and setting goals.

Career consultants, counselors, and coaches are good choices when you need help taking action in your career planning, job search, or ongoing career management.

Personal and Life Coaches

The term coach used to refer to the person on your neighborhood little league field wearing a whistle and a nervous expression or to the guy on the sidelines of an NFL game wearing a headset and looking like he needs a shot of Maalox. Now, the term coach doesn't necessarily have anything to do with sports. It can mean a personal or life coach: someone who helps you reach your goals.

Personal coaches are a little bit like psychotherapists, career counselors, executive coaches, and professional organizers; but at the same time, they are like none of them. They don't deal with the major emotional or psychological issues that psychotherapists handle, but they do provide a nonjudgmental forum for expressing your hopes, dreams, fears, and concerns. They don't always have the in-depth knowledge of career development that a career counselor has, but they can help you set and reach your professional goals. They don't usually roll up their sleeves and tear apart your closet or filing cabinets like professional organizers would, but they do help you get your act together and keep it together in a more general sense.

Coaches act as partners who help you take action. They often take a no-holds-barred, no-nonsense approach that keeps you focused on your target.

Although some coaches are certified by a credentialing organization, the personal coaching field is even more unregulated than the other counseling and coaching professions. Be sure to ask questions about your prospective coach's training, experience, and approach so you can make an informed decision about the coach you choose to work with.

MATTER OF FACT

If you've been putting off anything related to education, whether it's signing up your newborn for nursery school, finding a summer program for your special-needs teenager, or going back to college later in life, an independent educational consultant can help you and your family make the right choices. For information on how an educational consultant could help, or for referral to one near you, turn to the Independent Educational Consultants Association (IECA) at www.educationalconsulting.org.

Professional Organizers

Do you look at the piles of paper on your desk and feel like you'd rather throw them out the window than try to sort through and organize them yourself? Have you cleaned out your closets more times than you care to remember but find that they just get messy again soon after? It may be time to call in someone who declutters, files, organizes, and sets up systems for a living. Yes, such a person does exist and may be just what you need to get your life on track.

According to the National Association of Professional Organizers (www.napo.net), a professional organizer has the skills and experience to provide information, ideas, structure, solutions, and systems that increase productivity, reduce stress, and lead to more control over time, space, actions, and resources.

Professional organizers can work wonders and are important allies in the battle against procrastination.

Questions to Ask When Seeking Professional Help

The following questions can help you zero in on the best psycho-therapist, career counselor, coach, or professional organizer for your needs:

> What is the approach or philosophy behind your work?
>
> What can I expect to have happen when we first meet?
>
> Do you work on a session-by-session or hourly basis, or do I have to sign up for a package?
>
> Do you work on a one-on-one basis, in groups, or both?
>
> What is the average length of time someone would work with you to reach his or her goals?
>
> What is your professional background (education, work experience, and so on)?
>
> Do you have any licenses, certifications, or credentials? Are these required in your field and state, or are they optional?
>
> How long have you been in private practice or in your own consulting business?
>
> How much experience do you have dealing with people who have procrastination problems?
>
> Do you have a particular specialty or area of expertise?
>
> What do you charge for your services, and which forms of payment do you accept? Do you participate in any insurance plans?

No matter who ends up on your support team after you rally your family and friends or interview the professionals to find the right one to work with, the important thing is to have a support team. Getting and staying connected with people who can offer support, encouragement, advice, and resources is a critical element in your efforts to banish procrastination from your life.

The Least You Need to Know

- If you feel like you're not going to be able to stop procrastinating, it's probably because your past attempts failed.
- Understanding why your behavioral changes haven't worked in the past makes you less likely to repeat your mistakes.
- Change is difficult because it takes time and effort, it is hard to do alone, and it leads you into unfamiliar territory.
- You're much more likely to succeed at overcoming procrastination if you have the support of friends, family, and professional counselors or organizers.

The Path to Becoming an Ex-Procrastinator

Part

2

You've made it to Part 2, and you haven't given up yet. See, you don't put off everything. Your momentum should build even more as you read these next chapters because now you're getting to the really good stuff. This part is where I tell you exactly how you're going to stop procrastinating.

In Chapter 5 and Chapter 6, we'll look at how you're going to get your life under control so that you can set the stage for overcoming procrastination. You'll get rid of clutter, stop fighting with time, simplify your life, balance your commitments, and become organized so that no more obstacles stand in the way of getting things done.

In Chapter 7, you will learn how to become a whiz at decision-making, whether the decision is about what to have for dinner or what to do with your life. And in Chapter 8, you'll get a "prescription" for stopping procrastination before it takes over, as well as a simple, 10-step plan for getting things started and finishing what you start in any area of your life.

It's About Time— Finding, Using, and Enjoying It

In This Chapter

- How to stop fighting with time
- Finding time to get it all done
- Maintaining balance in life
- Learning to say no

Time exists. Period. Contrary to popular belief, it doesn't fly, drag, or accomplish any of the other feats we ascribe to it. You get 24 hours a day and 7 days a week whether you're Oprah Winfrey or Homer Simpson. If you live to be 90 years old, you'll get 47,304,000 minutes of time. It's your choice how you spend them. (And with that many minutes, you can waste a few now and then without feeling guilty!)

Why You Can't (and Shouldn't Want to) Manage Time

It's presumptuous of us to think we can manage time. After all, time has a lot to do with how the earth spins on its axis and revolves around the sun. Maybe Steven Spielberg or Angelina Jolie could have a go at it, but most of us mere mortals are powerless over forces of nature. We can't control time; all we can control is our behavior. We can conduct ourselves in a way that makes the most of the time we're given.

YOU'RE NOT ALONE

Time is man's most precious asset. All men neglect it; all regret the loss of it; nothing can be done without it.

—Voltaire, eighteenth-century French writer and historian

The fact that you can't manage or control time shouldn't come as a major disappointment. Do you want to think of your life as having to be "managed"? Life is to be lived, not managed.

ACTION TACTIC

It's a morbid thought, but imagine you found out you were going to die in one week. What would you regret about how you've spent your time up until now, and what would you do with the remaining time? Think about it and see if clues to your true priorities emerge.

Don't Be Bullied by Time

Some people are in a perpetual fight with time. They believe that it's not on their side or that it passes too quickly. Think about the colorful expressions some people use when describing how time pressures make them feel: spread too thin, pulled in too many directions, swamped, pressed, and pushed to the limit.

If you think time is out to get you, then it's no surprise that you also happen to be a procrastinator. The fight with time is a losing battle that distracts you from doing the things you need to do to deal with your problem.

Who Controls Your Time?

Do you sometimes feel you don't do the things you need or want to do because other people are controlling how you spend your time? Whether you feel pulled in too many directions by a spouse, kids, boss, friends, clients, or anyone else in your life, you might be putting off simple tasks or major dreams because others supposedly aren't letting you have the time you need.

Who *is* controlling your time? No one. That's right. Other people can make demands on your time, but they can't control it.

Making Peace with Time

An important step to becoming an ex-procrastinator is to make peace with time. Stop obsessing over how little you have or how quickly it passes. Own up to the fact that time simply exists. It's not out to get you, and it's up to you to make the most of it.

 QUICKSAND!

Don't run out of time when you could've prepared for a foreseeable crunch: Returning from vacation or a business trip means extra laundry and dry cleaning, plus unpacking. Coming off a busy weekend means you'll have household chores to catch up on. Meeting an important deadline means that other areas of your life have been neglected and will need your attention. Block time in your schedule to take care of any backlog you might face.

In *Stop Screaming at the Microwave: How to Connect Your Disconnected Life*, Mary LoVerde gives us a wake-up call with this statement:

> In mathematics, when you add and add and add without stopping it's called infinity. In life, when you add and add and add without stopping it's called insanity. Something's gotta go.

Even though this book is all about getting things done, I don't want you to think for a minute that it's only about getting more done. Your aim should be to do the important things, not just more things. It's about quality of life, not quantity of tasks.

How Not to Be Handcuffed to Your Calendar

Being a slave to your calendar—whether digital, paper, or scrawled on your wrist—is one of the ways you might be trying to do too much. As the pace of life has picked up in recent years due to technological, workplace, and societal changes, many people crowd their calendars with more tasks and engagements than any human being can reasonably handle.

Making the most of time is not a matter of piling on the obligations or rigidly scheduling your days. A life that is nothing more than appointments written into a day planner or items on a to-do list fuels procrastination. It does so by making you feel that you're in a rut, that your life is overly regimented, and that life is nothing more than a collection of obligations to meet. This routine can bring about feelings of resentment, stress, and burnout—emotions that fuel procrastination.

QUICKSAND!

Multitasking (taking care of two or more obligations or chores simultaneously) can be a good way to make the most of your time, but watch out for hidden dangers in this strategy. You might not do as good a job with the individual tasks because you're dividing your attention, and you may start to feel burned out if you're always tackling too much at once.

Stop Using the "But I Just Can't Find the Time" Excuse

You know that I'm not trying to turn you into a workhorse who never has any fun, and you understand that you determine how you spend your time. But you can't quite buy into the concept that not only will you be able to get your big responsibilities and routine tasks taken care of, you'll also have time left over to kick back and contemplate your navel or whatever else you'd choose to do with some free time. You can barely find the time to get yourself and the kids (or yourself and the houseplants) fed and watered each day. How will you ever find time to catch up on all the things that have piled up while you've been procrastinating? You can't get things done because you just can't find the time. Or so you say.

Isn't it interesting that you can almost always find the time to do things that are easy or enjoyable? You can while away two hours on a Saturday afternoon watching a classic movie on television, but you can't find 30 minutes to weed the garden. You find time to check Facebook but can't find time to answer an email.

It seems to be human nature that most people, especially procrastinators, do the things that are fun or easy first. When you develop the habit of procrastinating, you act on impulse rather than thinking through your actions. Your impulses often point you to the quickest, most pleasant activity rather than the more difficult or complex ones.

People often neglect their long-range plans and ambitions or current priorities because they spend too much time responding to what's urgent or pressing. Suppose that your two top priorities in life right now are to get physically fit and to spend more quality time with your family or friends. But no matter how important those goals are to you, your daily actions don't reflect them.

You have high hopes of exercising at least a few days a week after work, but you keep getting waylaid by last-minute crises that pop up on the job. You want to go on an outing every weekend with the kids (or friends) for a healthy dose of fun and maybe even some culture or education, but you don't plan enough ahead to make it happen. Or you become sidetracked by household chores that have to be done by Monday.

Getting Your Priorities Straight

Unless you plan in advance and put some organizational and procedural systems in place at home and work, you'll spend all your time responding to the pressing needs of the moment and will never get around to doing the things that relate to your true priorities and long-term goals.

You may say that developing that sideline business is a priority, but you never seem to have time to work on it in the evenings. You may say that searching online for old friends you've lost touch with is a priority, but every time you get on, you only have time to do your business for the day, not to search for them.

The key is to determine on any given day or any particular moment whether the time is right to focus on the big-picture, overarching goals you have in life or whether a more mundane task needs to be the priority.

ACTION TACTIC

Close your eyes and picture time. What do you see? Do you see a clock, a calendar, or a long, straight line? Do you see people and places? Do you picture the future or the past? There's no one correct mental image of time or one best way to interpret what you see. It's just an interesting exercise that might clue you in to your relationship with time.

Banish the "It's Not the Right Time to Do This" Excuse

For some procrastinators, the problem is not so much that they don't have the time but that the time isn't right. They're waiting for a day when the boss is in a good mood, the temperature is 72°F, the kids are with a sitter, they feel motivated and energetic, and the heavens part.

YOU'RE NOT ALONE

Dost thou love life? Then do not waste time, for that is the stuff life is made of.

—Benjamin Franklin, eighteenth-century American statesman and inventor

Procrastinators who wait for the right time to do something are often waiting for the perfect time—a time that doesn't exist. As I said in Chapter 1, there is such a thing as good procrastination, consciously putting off something because it makes legitimate sense to do so. But many procrastinators abuse that principle and turn it into a contingency excuse, the excuse that they can't do one thing until some other chain of events occurs. When this excuse is used, productive action rarely takes place, because even if conditions do become just about right, another contingency always seems to come along.

Creating the Illusion of More Time

Whether you don't have enough time or can't find the right time, you probably wish there were 25 hours (or more) in each day. You can feel like you have more time by trying these tricks:

- **Focus on the moment.** Time doesn't seem to go by so quickly when you fully live in the present moment, instead of going through the motions of life not focusing on what you're doing.

- **Simplify.** The less clutter and fewer commitments you have, the less you'll feel pulled in so many different directions.

- **Delegate.** Short of cloning yourself, delegating is the best way to get twice as much done in a limited period of time. Turning projects and chores over to others saves you time and energy.

- **Develop systems.** If you feel like you waste a lot of time putting out fires, those crises and urgent matters that arise at home or work, you need to put organizational, management, and procedural systems in place so that those fires eventually stop igniting.

- **Slow down.** The more you bite off, the longer you have to chew. If you keep adding things to your to-do list and taking on more responsibilities in your life roles, you're going to feel as though the days are shorter and time is running out.

- **Enjoy quiet.** Build into your day some quiet times that serve as mini-escapes from the world. These are times when you turn down the volume (literally and figuratively), go off by yourself, and relax. You might shut your eyes, take off your shoes and wiggle your toes, and take some deep breaths. Do whatever you need to do to relax and rejuvenate.

- **Don't worry about what's next.** If you are continually thinking about what you have to do next or how much work is left on a particular project, you'll create the sensation of time speeding up. You'll forget about the time you do have left and will start worrying that you're running out of time.

Now that you have an idea of how you might adopt new ways of thinking about time, let's look at how you're going to handle getting things done within the time you have.

Why To-Do Lists Don't Get Done—and What You Can Do

I keep a personal to-do list, which is separate from my work-related list. Every time I write something on my work-related list, I schedule a day and sometimes a specific time to do each task by entering it in my calendar online. The method works, and I get things done. But when I'm in a crunch to meet work deadlines or have a particularly heavy work to-do list, my personal to-do list tends to get neglected. I write things on the personal list so that I won't forget to do them eventually, but I am not very diligent about scheduling specific days or times for getting them done.

ACTION TACTIC

Put trash cans around your house where you don't typically think of having them, such as the living room, dining room, or hallways. (Buy or make attractive ones if you're worried about wrecking the decor.) Having a trash can handy at all times makes you more likely to throw out papers and stuff you don't need, making it easier to take action on the things you do keep.

To-do lists—work or personal—are useless if you don't do two things:

1. Look at them frequently. That may sound like the most obvious advice in the world, but many people take the time to make elaborate lists and then never give them a second glance. If you're guilty of that, you probably tend to forget about things that need to be dealt with.

2. Designate times when you'll do the things on the list. To-do lists are merely inventories. By glancing at a list, you see what you need to do; you check inventory. Lists do not, however, spark action. To get things done, take each item on the list and mark it in your calendar.

We all also have things in life that are ongoing tasks—household chores, routine responsibilities at work, and annual events such as medical check-ups. We don't usually put these on a to-do list because they are always in the back of our minds as things we need to take care of. To make sure these actions don't get stuck in the musty recesses of your mind and actually get done, you need to put some routines in place.

The Beauty of Routine

A routine is a wonderful thing. By knowing that the second Tuesday of every month is the day you pay bills, you don't have to spend all the other days of the month worrying and saying things like, "I should probably be paying some bills." A routine tells you what to do and when to do it. Although that may sound constricting, it's actually liberating. A routine frees you up to enjoy life or at least not to stress out over things. If you know that you regularly do certain tasks on certain days of the week or month, maybe even at specific times, or that you designate certain dates of the year to handle annual responsibilities, you don't have to think about those things at other times.

Think about all the things you have to do on an ongoing basis, particularly those you tend to put off doing, and designate days you'll do them routinely. That way, they won't nag at you daily or weekly. You free yourself up not to think about them other than on the day you're supposed to do them.

QUICKSAND!

Don't crowd your to-do list with tasks that you have no intention of doing in the remotely near future. Being overly ambitious and filling your list with nonessential tasks will only make you feel guilty and unproductive (when you don't do them), which might keep you from doing the important things. Keep a separate list of backburner projects and long-range goals.

The Gentle Art of Scheduling

I call scheduling a gentle art, because we have to go easy on ourselves when filling our calendars. Sure, there are days when we really have to pack in the appointments and to-do items. But by making scheduling a gentle art, you stay conscious of the need to build in some down time, some time for taking care of unexpected flare-ups, or just to get another glass of water. To do this, consider these guidelines:

- Have a routine schedule for the weekly chores and appointments you regularly have.

- Whenever you schedule a nonroutine appointment, think through every step that it would involve: advance preparation, getting ready on the day of the appointment, travel time, and so on. Then schedule it on a day and time when you know you can get through all the steps with a minimum amount of hassle and allow enough time for all the steps.

- Consult other key people, such as co-workers, friends, or family, before scheduling. It does you no good to arrange a meeting or social engagement only to find that the time is no good for others who need to be involved.

- Keep your overall priorities and goals in mind when scheduling your day-to-day action. For example, writing a thank-you note might be a priority, but is a particular work deadline a bigger priority?

- Maintain balance in your life. Don't schedule every minute of the day. Allow some time to be spontaneous and do nothing (or to do something fun on the spur of the moment). If your life is extremely busy, you might have to build balance into your schedule. Scheduled spontaneity is better than none at all.

- Work with your natural rhythms. Don't schedule a workout at 6 A.M. if you're not a morning person. Don't plan to make cold calls after lunch if that's the time of day you feel most sluggish. Use your common sense and schedule routine tasks or occasional appointments at times that make sense for your energy level.

As you work on your routine schedules and spruce up your calendar, you should be getting a sense of where your life might be out of whack in terms of following priorities, working toward goals, and achieving balance. One factor causing this could be commitment overload. Let's look at how you can deal with that.

> **ACTION TACTIC**
>
> Always tell yourself that an appointment or event is half an hour before it is. Even though you'll know the real time, if you keep that real time pushed far enough to the back of your mind, you'll forget about it and will start to think that the fake, earlier time is the actual one.

Balancing Acts

Not all clutter is the kind that grows in your closet or your monitor's desktop. You can also get slowed down by a glut of obligations in any of your life roles.

Suppose you're moving along in your daily routine, managing to get everything done, when something comes along and upsets the apple cart. Perhaps you have to care for an elderly relative or a family member who suddenly becomes sick or injured. This happens at the same time that you're nearing critical deadlines at work, remodeling your kitchen, trying to stick with an exercise plan, and devoting energy to a new romantic relationship in your life. Just when you thought you had your act together, a case of commitment overload kicks in.

Some commitments, such as those related to unexpected illness, are difficult, if not impossible, to control. Others, however, like pointless meetings you're asked to attend, committees you get volunteered for, household projects you ambitiously take on, are within your control. You can say no!

Why It's Hard to Say No

If you find yourself too often saying yes to obligations that end up eating up your time and making you feel stressed, then you need to figure out why it's so difficult to say no. Check off the following reasons that ring true for you, and then start using the strategies suggested after the ones you checked:

❐ Your sense of duty compels you to take on any obligation that comes your way.

Strategy: You can be of more service to people if you carefully pick and choose your commitments so that you have enough time and energy to devote to each one. Remember that you also have a duty to treat yourself well—not just other people!

❐ You want to be liked.

Strategy: Are people going to dislike you if you decline their invitations or requests? In most cases, people take a no much more easily than you expect them to. But people won't be too thrilled if you take on something you don't want to do or that you can't commit to fully.

❐ You like to feel needed.

Strategy: It's nice to feel that others rely on you, but commitment is a quality issue, not a quantity one. You don't have to overextend yourself to feel needed. Instead, focus on the satisfaction you get from devoting your time and energy to a select group of people and organizations, and don't let yourself get spread too thin.

❐ You want to avoid confrontation.

Strategy: It's very unlikely that anyone is going to yell and scream and stomp his or her feet when you say no to a request for your time. Telling someone no isn't necessarily the most pleasant exchange you'll ever have, but it's not likely to trigger World War III.

❏   You feel flattered to be asked.

Strategy: Flattery doesn't bring 25 or 35 hours to your day. Not far behind that warm and fuzzy feeling you get from the flattery is the resentment you'll feel over the time and effort you have to put into a particular project. If it's flattery you need, tell your loved ones to say nice things to you more often.

❏   You're afraid to miss out on something.

Strategy: If honoring the request is practically guaranteed to propel you closer to your personal or career goals, then do it. If not, realize that if this opportunity came along, then there will probably be more like it down the road.

❏   You're losing sight of reality.

Strategy: Some demands for your time are presented as quick and easy little blips on the calendar. If you tend to fall for vague promises that a particular project won't disrupt your life or take up much of your time, then you need to be more careful when the request is made. Think through the day-to-day reality of what this obligation would entail and what it would do to your life.

Once you understand why the word yes rolls off your tongue far too often, you'll be ready to start replacing yes with no.

How to Say No

To say no painlessly and politely, follow these rules:

- Keep your priorities in mind at all times. If a request for your time doesn't fit in with your values and goals, you should probably say no.

- If you know right away that you don't have the desire or time to do something, turn down the request as soon as possible. The longer you wait, the more likely you are to back down and change your mind, and the more difficult it will be for the other person to find someone else to do it.

- When you're asked to take on a particular commitment, if your first reaction is uncertainty, don't decide immediately. Never let anyone rush you. Take the time you need to think through all the possible consequences of doing the project.

- Ask other people for input on your decision. If you decide to decline the offer, you'll feel more confident in saying so because you didn't make the decision alone.

- Say no in a succinct but polite way. Giving too much detail about your situation opens the door for the other person to try to find ways to fit the obligation into your schedule. Simply say you'd like to do it, or that you're flattered by the offer, but your schedule does not allow it.

Remember that no matter how difficult it may be to say no, it's much easier to do so before you've committed to something than to bow out after the fact.

ACTION TACTIC

If there's no way to get out of a project you've already committed to and you no longer can find the time to do it, try to delegate as many tasks as possible to someone else to ease your burden.

The beauty of overcoming procrastination is that you'll enjoy life more. By getting routine chores taken care of, major responsibilities met, and backburner projects out of the way, you free up time to pursue activities that you find rewarding, fun, or relaxing. You can spend more time making meaningful connections with people, places, and things rather than merely going through the motions of life.

The Least You Need to Know

- Time can't be controlled or managed. You can only control how you use it.
- Overcoming procrastination is not about packing more commitments into your schedule or chores onto your to-do list.
- Taking care of responsibilities and routine tasks frees you up to do things that bring you enjoyment and satisfaction.
- Saying no to requests for your time is easier than you might think.

Decluttering and Organizing

In This Chapter

- Take stock of your clutter crisis
- Experience the freedom that comes from dejunking
- Find the proverbial safe place for things
- Low-tech and high-tech organizing options
- Where to put all that paper

You don't have to be the woman with 153 cats slinking around her house, or the man with a neatly arranged collection of 60,000 beer cans, or the guy who has to live in a trailer in the backyard because he can't get inside his house due to the piles of debris, to have a clutter crisis—or even a clutter problem.

Serious hoarding is no laughing matter—hoarders are usually suffering from unfortunate psychological disorders—but we do tend to make jokes out of the mindboggling stories we hear or see on television about people whose lives are overcome with stuff. We think we're nothing like them. I don't mean to scare you into thinking you're heading down that path if you've saved a month's worth of mail on your kitchen counter. But even a minor clutter or organization problem can lead to a major procrastination problem. Clean, uncluttered spaces encourage action. If your dresser drawers weren't so crowded, you probably wouldn't procrastinate about putting away clean laundry. If your file cabinets weren't so stuffed with useless papers, and if you had a user-friendly filing system, you'd be more likely to get back to those great business ideas buried within them. The fewer obstacles standing in the way, the more likely you are to be productive.

Assessing Your Clutter Crisis

The first step in getting rid of clutter (the physical kind: papers, objects, and miscellaneous stuff) is to take stock of where it is. You know which closet you'd hate to have a guest open accidentally, because your insurance might not cover the head injury caused by flying objects. You know which kitchen drawer always gets jammed by all the useless utensils you've been collecting for decades.

To find out where all your clutter hotspots are, the obvious and not-so-obvious ones, walk yourself (either literally or mentally) through each room of your home or each area of your office. Make a list of your top 10 clutter problem areas. Be fairly specific, such as "the hall closet," or "the shelves on the back garage wall." When you're that specific, you probably can't fit every problem area into a top 10 list, but you keep your list manageable. Clearing out the whole garage right now might seem too daunting, but focusing only on a certain section of it is likely to be doable. You can always move on to other problem spots once you've tackled the first 10.

How to Stop Rationalizing Your Clutter Habit

Think of all the excuses you come up with for letting clutter accumulate:

- I'm just a packrat. It's how I am.
- I might need this someday.
- I'll be able to fit into this again when I lose weight.
- It will come back in style.
- I have special memories connected to this.

- I paid too much for this to just throw it out or give it away.

- They don't make them like this anymore.

- I might be able to fix this and make it like new.

- This was a gift, so it would be wrong of me to get rid of it.

Occasionally these statements are valid. Maybe you can repair something and get some use out of it again. Maybe you just have to keep some gifts no matter how much you dislike them or how little need you have for them. Perhaps your diet and exercise program really is melting off the pounds weekly.

In most cases, though, these statements are nothing more than excuses for keeping your life in disarray. If you want to become more productive, stop using excuses like these. Keeping yourself surrounded by too much stuff in every nook and cranny of your home or office is like wrapping yourself in a warm, cozy blanket. The clutter protects you. It provides an excuse for not having to get on with life.

Where Your Attachment to Stuff Comes From

To stop making excuses for a clutter habit, you have to know why you make them in the first place. I can't just tell you to stop saying something like "This is too valuable to throw out." You'll come up with 10 more arguments to make sure you don't have to get rid of that allegedly valuable item. The only way you're going to stop making these excuses is to understand the psychology behind them or the circumstances that have led to them. Your reasons for keeping things probably fall into several basic categories.

The following sections detail the categories and provide examples of each of these reasons along with solutions for dealing with your rationalizations.

Guilt

So you paid hundreds of dollars for that fancy kitchen mixer, but the closest you've come to baking a cake from scratch is defrosting one of Sara Lee's finest. Even so, you can't bring yourself to give it away despite the fact that you curse it every time you see how much counter or cabinet space it takes up. Or maybe there are tools, clothes, exercise equipment, or something else you paid an arm and a leg for but haven't gotten more than a week's use out of. You feel guilty for spending money on things you aren't using, so you keep them around to trick yourself into believing that they were worthwhile purchases.

It's not just the big-ticket items that cause the guilt, either. Maybe you tend to make impulse purchases while waiting in the check-out line of stores. If you threw out all the useless little trinkets and gadgets you've accumulated that way, you'd be admitting that they were foolish purchases.

Guilt also plays a role when you've received gifts that you don't like or need. It seems ungrateful to get rid of something that was a gift, so you keep it out of guilt.

> **ACTION TACTIC**
>
> If you tend to hoard stuff and have limited space, then follow this rule: every time you bring something new into your home (anything from a magazine, to an item of clothing, a piece of furniture, or whatever), discard or give away something comparable that's already there.

Finally, you might be keeping things because you feel guilty about having what others don't have. Maybe you're unwilling to throw out that can of fruit cocktail that's been sitting in your cupboard for eight years because you feel bad for the starving kids in some country halfway around the world. Never mind that you and no one you know likes canned fruit cocktail and you don't know how you ended up with it in the first place.

Here's the solution: stop buying things you don't need. If you have a problem with impulse buying, make yourself put more thought into each purchase. You can even consider adopting a cash-only policy, which makes it more difficult to buy things than if you were just whipping out a credit or debit card. If your shopping in general is out of control, admit it and seek professional help.

Also, tell people who regularly give you or your family gifts to stop doing so. Realize that letting a gift sit around unused and unappreciated is just as bad as giving it away or throwing it out, so you may as well get rid of it. If you're worried about people less fortunate than you, then pack up your food, clothes, or whatever and send it to them, or drop your donation off at a local soup kitchen or shelter.

QUICKSAND!

Online auctions, consumer-to-consumer sites such as Craigslist, and other e-commerce venues make it easier than ever to acquire stuff. Plus popular television shows such as *Antiques Roadshow* have made us more aware of the money-making potential of antiques and collectibles. Don't let all this turn you into a packrat just because you think your junk might be a treasure some day. Save only what has a good chance of being valuable currently or in the future. And if it isn't particularly high in monetary value, make sure you love it!

Value

"I'm keeping this because it might be worth a lot of money one day." How many times have you made (or heard) that excuse? Do you really think that pile of old magazines gathering dust in the corner is likely to turn into a treasure trove of rare journalism and let you retire a millionaire? Holding on to items you don't use, enjoy, or gain any current value from is a common mistake of packrats.

Here's the solution: if you're keeping things because they might be worth some money in the future, verify that assumption. Do the necessary research to find out how likely it is that your junk will turn to gold. If experts tell you it's a long shot, you probably don't have much to lose by discarding it.

ACTION TACTIC

If you find yourself reluctant to throw things out, think about people who lose everything in a major fire or tornado. No matter how devastating their loss of material possessions, most people say that they're just thankful that they and their loved ones are alive. Think about how much stuff you have and how trivial its loss would be compared with the loss of a loved one. I bet you'll find a few things you can throw out or give away!

Sentimentality

Keeping things for sentimental reasons is hard to argue with. I'm notorious for wanting to save every wedding invitation, birth announcement, and holiday card I receive, as well as ticket stubs from favorite concerts, playbills from theater outings, knick-knacks collected on trips, and just about anything else that is fun or touches me in some way. Then there are the purple suede ballet flats I bought in Florence, Italy, in 1987; I held onto them for 20 years, long after they became worn beyond repair, because they were the most fabulous pair of shoes I'd ever owned.

I'm sure you have your own items you can't seem to part with. Old photographs, correspondence, souvenirs, and other keepsakes are important reminders of special people, places, and things in our lives. I'm the last person to tell you to chuck it all and live a totally unsentimental life. But there comes a point when you have to remind yourself what the word keepsake means. You have to ask yourself what the sake, or purpose, is for keeping something. If it is near and dear to your heart, and having the physical object is the only way to preserve it, then by all means keep it. If not, it might be time to part company.

Before you rationalize that everything is near and dear to your heart and must be kept physically, consider this compromise: find ways to preserve the memory of events, people, things, or places without having to use up valuable space storing every physical reminder of them. You can take a photo of yourself holding or wearing something you're going to throw out or give away. You can scan any paper items and store them digitally. You can keep a journal in which you write about special events so that you don't have to save the ticket stub, the program, and the parking lot receipt. If the silly paper hat you wore during Mardi Gras in 1986 is so special to you, frame it and hang it on the wall.

As for those things you want to save but that don't fit or belong in scrapbooks, or that really need to be kept in original form rather than scanned, keep the amount manageable by limiting how much memorabilia you allow yourself to save each year. Designate no more than one box per year as a memorabilia box that you can put things in throughout the year, then store it away in your attic, garage, or a closet.

Time-Capsule Syndrome

Related to the sentimentality excuse for keeping things is what I call the time-capsule syndrome. Not only might you save things because they have emotional value for you, but you are also determined to save them for that proverbial posterity, for some sort of historical value. According to *Webster's New World Dictionary*, posterity means "all of a person's descendants" or "all future generations."

As with sentimentality, there's nothing wrong with saving some things that will capture a moment in time for your grandkids or for future generations not even related to you. As our society's communication and creative expression become more and more digital, and therefore not often saved in any physical form we can touch and hold, it is important that we all do our part to keep some record of our times for future generations to learn from or just have a laugh over. The problem comes when you start saving anything and everything and the items become clutter rather than carefully chosen time-markers.

YOU'RE NOT ALONE

One of the most touching examples I ever heard of a wonderful sentimental excuse for saving junk was the story of a man who was clearing out his deceased parents' garage. The parents, who had died within six months of each other, were Depression-era people who saved everything. The son and his sisters put most of the parents' saved odds and ends into several commercial dumpsters they'd rented for the clean-out. But there was one item they couldn't part with that the son took home to keep on his mantel—a cigar box that his mother had carefully labeled "Pieces of string too short to use."

Here's the solution: if something is worth saving for posterity, then it shouldn't be stuck in a box somewhere; it should be on display to be enjoyed and remembered or, if put away, at least be labeled and easily accessible.

Practicality

Some people are practical to the point of impracticality. They save every spare part, scrap of food, bit of cloth, torn sock, and anything else that could come in handy some day. This behavior is often typical of people who lived through hard times or who emigrated from a country where resources were scarce.

There's nothing wrong with not wanting to be wasteful, but keeping so many odds and ends on hand slows you down. You end up fishing through drawers filled with bits and pieces of what is essentially junk to the point where you can't find what's not junk.

Here's the solution: every time you're about to save something in the name of practicality, pause and ask yourself what the chances are that you will fix, use, or need that item. Also, think through the consequences of not saving it. Could you replace it easily? Do you already have a duplicate? Being practical is a good habit, but like all good habits, it can be taken to the extreme.

Hopes and Dreams

You thought you were going to start a home-based business, but the idea fizzled out. Now you're left with all sorts of papers and books from the research you did and maybe even some inventory if you had progressed that far. Or perhaps you took some graduate school courses but gave up hope of completing a degree and now can't seem to part with the textbooks and notes that take up valuable bookshelf space. Or maybe you had planned to lose weight and get fit, but your wardrobe of smaller clothes and unused exercise equipment just gathers dust.

Some hopes and dreams may not be major life-changing goals like those just described but are small projects you thought you'd get to someday: the sweater you planned to knit, the chair seat you thought you'd re-cane all by yourself, the videos you were going to watch, or the cheerful holiday cards you planned to turn into a collage. Projects like these start out with the best of intentions but usually fall victim to the realities and demands of daily life. What you end up with is lots of stuff around you that could have been put to good use but instead becomes clutter.

Here's the solution: prevent the problem before it starts. Before you accumulate paraphernalia, think carefully about the likelihood that you will carry out the project or work toward that goal. As for the things you've already collected, be realistic about how likely you are to use them.

If your clutter relates to significant unfinished projects, such as abandoned business ideas or personal goals, parting with the remnants of those lost dreams can be more difficult psychologically. The best way to let go of that type of clutter is to realize that everyone has unfulfilled goals. There's nothing wrong with that. You're only making matters worse by keeping the painful reminders around. By throwing them out, you free yourself to move on to new pursuits.

 YOU'RE NOT ALONE

I added to my clutter problem by buying a sewing machine that has sat unopened in its original box through two house moves, gathering dust and taking up space. I don't know what made me think I'd run up some curtains or make costumes for my son when I don't really even know how to sew, don't particularly enjoy it, and surely don't have time for it on top of a full-time job and chasing after a 2-year-old.

—Joanna H., pension fund manager

Identity

Some of us keep certain objects around because we draw our identity from them. The possessions we choose to surround ourselves with tell other people, as well as ourselves, who we are or who we'd like to be (or even who we used to be). We don't necessarily use these things or even get much enjoyment from them, but we feel tied to them, so we keep them.

> **QUICKSAND!**
>
> Don't buy something simply because it's on sale or because you have a coupon for it. Put thought into every purchase; otherwise, you're just accumulating clutter.

Think about the things you might be keeping around because you like what they say about you. Then think about the inconvenience, if any, that they're causing. Do they take up space you could use for something else? Do you have to dust around them? Do you waste time sorting through them to get to what you need? Are they necessary to have on hand?

Here's the solution: realize that you are not your stuff. Your identity comes from what you do, not what you have on your bookshelves or on the walls of your office. There's no harm in keeping a few things around that tell the world "This is what I like and what's important to me." If we didn't, we'd be boring people living and working in boring surroundings. But when you could use the space for other purposes, it might be time to weed out your collections.

Getting Rid of Stuff

You know what you've been accumulating too much of and why you've done it. Now you have to get rid of it. Yes, you really have to.

> **ACTION TACTIC**
>
> If you find it difficult to give away or throw out unused items that are nice and maybe even pricey, consider donating them to a charitable group that could use them in a silent auction.

First, start an anti-clutter notebook to keep on hand while you clean out various spaces. Use it to make note of items you need to return to someone, things that need to be repaired, and supplies you need to buy or find to organize an area or make necessary repairs. Also, schedule times to take action on the tasks you've written in your anti-clutter notebook. For example, get out your appointment book or electronic calendar and enter that next Saturday you will go buy storage bins to organize the remaining sweaters in your closet.

To start ridding yourself of clutter, choose just one small area or one set of like items to clear out at any given time. One area might mean a single drawer, one pile of papers, the top shelf of a closet, or the tool wall of your garage. Don't try to tackle too much at once. Clearing out one small space will give you the incentive to go on and do the rest. Also, set aside a realistic amount of time to start and complete the project. Schedule it for a firm date and time as if it were an important engagement.

If you think you're going to have a struggle disciplining yourself to keep the appointment or getting rid of things once the time comes, ask someone to work on the project with you, or at least have them "chaperone" you. Just make sure that person is not a packrat!

When it comes time to clean up the area you selected, set up and label sorting containers (boxes or trash bags) that you will put stuff in. You should have one container for each of the following categories:

- **To Keep: Easy** (for things that have a place and will be easy to put away)

- **To Keep: Difficult** (for things that you will need to find or create a place for)

- **To Repair** (for things you need to repair yourself, have someone fix for you, or take or mail in for repair)

- **To Scan** (for papers, photos, and other items you want to save digitally before throwing out the physical item)

- **To Return** (for borrowed items)

- **To Trash** (for things you can throw away)

- **To Recycle** (for glass, aluminum, paper, and other recyclables)

- **To Give Away** (for things you'll donate to charity or give to other people)

- **To Sell** (for items you can sell online, through a newspaper ad, or in a future garage sale)

- **Not Sure** (for items that aren't easy to categorize right away)

YOU'RE NOT ALONE

When I was a kid, my parents used to send me out to the garage to bundle up old newspapers for recycling. Eight hours later, I'd still be there reading the papers instead of preparing them for recycling!

—John H., psychologist

Go through one item at a time and put it in the appropriate box. To build some momentum, start by doing the easiest sorting first, such as throwing out things that you can get rid of without a second thought. Don't stop to read, reminisce over, try on, or otherwise be distracted by items you're sorting through. If you need more time to look something over before deciding whether to keep or discard it, put it in the Not Sure box. Just don't let everything end up in that box!

ACTION TACTIC

As an incentive to declutter your surroundings, calculate the cost of your home or office per square foot and estimate the square footage devoted to items you don't use, wear, or enjoy. How much is it costing you to store your clutter? What else could you be doing with that space if it were emptied out or less crowded?

When you rid your life of possessions that bring little or no joy or satisfaction, you lift an enormous weight off your shoulders. If you're a packrat now, you may find it hard to imagine life without all your stuff, but I guarantee that decluttering your surroundings will be a liberating experience and will make it easier to get organized in general.

A Crash Course in Getting Organized

Getting organized is not only an art and a science, it's also a booming industry. There are people who make a living wading through and sorting out other people's stuff and helping them get their acts together. There are also plenty of books with tips on how to clear off your desk or clean out your closets and any number of seminars that motivate you to make the most of your time.

The varying advice on getting organized presents a confusing array of choices. The important thing to remember is that there is no right or wrong way to organize. Sure, some techniques and systems are typically more effective than others, but organizing is a personal thing. You have to take all the expert advice and use the parts of it that work for you.

The Complete Idiot's Guide to Overcoming Procrastination, Second Edition, is not a book on organizing per se (there's *The Complete Idiot's Guide to Organizing Your Life* for that). What I offer here are some tips on the key elements of an organized life:

- **Find a place for everything and keep it there.** Your stuff gets messy because the places it's supposed to go are too crowded or aren't arranged conveniently, or maybe there's no designated place at all. Instead of continuing to trip over things, make a place for them and keep them there.

- **When possible, handle paper only once.** Take care of it immediately if the paper calls for you to respond, register, share it with someone, or take some other quick action. Or if you don't need to deal with it and don't need to keep it, throw it out!

- **Set up a "holding pattern" spot for papers you can't take action on right away.** Use plastic, metal, or wicker stacking trays or a hanging file folder stand with the following categories: To take action; To file; To pay; To scan; To read. Instead of letting papers pile up while waiting for time to do something with them, sort them into the appropriate tray or folder.

- **Keep a pending papers file or "in" basket.** We all collect things we need to hold on to for a while but won't need to keep forever, such as receipts, order confirmations, invitations, and more. Until you get to the point where all of these are in your smartphone and you don't have any more slips of paper here and there, you need one easy place—a file folder, box, or basket—to drop them in. Just be sure to clean it out regularly!

Whether your organizational downfall lies in the mounds of paper you feel you're drowning in or in other types of physical stuff—household items, clothes, office materials, sports equipment, or anything that slows you down—the trick is to pare it all down to the essentials, make sure it all has a place, and keep it where it belongs.

QUICKSAND!

Make sure that all other members of your household know where various items belong. In an emergency, it does no good for you to be the only one who knows that the flashlight is kept in the drawer to the left of the dishwasher.

The Least You Need to Know

- Before you can get organized and stop procrastinating, you have to simplify your life by getting rid of unnecessary possessions.
- Watch out for lame excuses you use to hang on to stuff.
- When you don't have a place for everything or don't keep things in their places, not only do your surroundings become messy, but you also get slowed down when you're trying to get things done.
- To deal with all the paper that comes your way, use stacking trays or hanging file folders to sort it into categories.

Make Better Decisions to Take Better Action

In This Chapter

- Decision-making: innate talent or learned skill?
- Why we make decisions harder than they need to be
- Identifying your decision-making style
- Deciding like a pro

Ann is a conscientious mother who wanted to find a good preschool for her son. She kept putting off enrolling him somewhere because she was waiting for the perfect option. She extended her search so long that she missed all the deadlines and had to send him to a school that was near the bottom of her list.

Donny is a magazine editor living in New York City where it costs an arm, a leg, and a kidney to rent an apartment. Thirteen years ago, Donny had the opportunity to get on a waiting list for a nice building known for its extremely reasonable rents and spacious apartments, a waiting list you could wait on for several years before you got to the top. At that time, he put off adding his name to the list because he was in the process of deciding whether he wanted to settle down in Manhattan permanently or move somewhere else. It took him so long to decide to stay that, as he now realizes, if he'd been more decisive, he could have been living in a nice, large apartment by now instead of in an overpriced one-room studio that doesn't even have a closet!

Why You Just Can't Decide

When you put off making a decision, you put your life on hold. You miss out on opportunities, have to settle for second best, and disappoint yourself as well as the people around you.

As with getting organized, decision-making is related to procrastination in two ways:

1. Decision-making may be the thing you procrastinate about. You delay making decisions that are difficult, take time, or have a lot riding on them. You wait until the very last minute to commit yourself to one direction or another.

2. Delayed decision-making may lead to procrastination in other areas of your life. Decision-making is at the root of action, so the things you put off doing might get put off because you can't decide when, how, or where to do them.

Whether the decision is a major life choice or merely a choice of what to do in the course of your workday or what to have for dinner, decision-making is often one of the biggest sources of frustration and confusion for procrastinators.

QUICKSAND!

If you dwell on the poor choices, you'll never develop the confidence you need to make good choices. Just because decisions you made in the past didn't work out so well, don't assume you're doomed to keep making the same mistakes.

Decisions are sometimes difficult to make because we've never learned how to make them. We rely on hit-or-miss methods that work if we're lucky or lead us down the wrong paths if we're not so fortunate. We don't realize that decision-making is a skill that can be learned. We become frustrated and disappointed in ourselves when we don't come by decision-making naturally.

In "The Eight Decision-Making Styles" later in this chapter, you'll learn how your own approach to decision-making might be at the root of the problem. Then in "Ten Steps to Decision-Making Like a Pro," you'll learn a simple decision-making method that I bet no one has ever taught you. For now, though, let's look at four other reasons why you may be stymied by your choices:

- You have too many choices and too much information.

- You have too few good choices or too little time or money to act on any.

- You make the decision harder than it needs to be.

- You're grappling with the identity issues that decision-making raises.

As with most instances of procrastination, putting off making decisions usually results from a combination of psychological and circumstantial factors. In other words, the options you have to choose from (the circumstances) and how you deal with those options (the psychology of decision-making) can create one whopper of an indecision dilemma.

Too Many Choices and Too Much Information

Think about any purchase you might need to make: a car, a phone, a piece of furniture, or anything at all. No matter what the item is, you probably have more products to choose from and more consumer information at your fingertips than at any time in history. You can go online and find hundreds or thousands of references to the product in question. There are sites that want to sell you the product, sites that warn you about the brands not to buy, sites with objective consumer information about several of your choices, and review sites where people are ranting and raving about the product at this very moment.

It can be more than a little overwhelming, particularly if you're the type of person who finds that even just one issue of *Consumer Reports* contains more information than you can handle. The fact that you can get not only every back issue of that magazine online but millions of other resources as well is mind-boggling.

This abundance is also overwhelming for those other people who believe that you can't have too much information before making a decision and who enjoy the research process a little too much. They might wander off into research never-never land and not come back to make the decision they set out to make.

ACTION TACTIC

Think of at least one good decision you've made in the past. Why did it turn out so well? What can you do to repeat the same success with a decision you currently need to make?

Not Enough Choices, Time, or Money

Sometimes tough decision-making is not a matter of too much, but too little. You might, for example, experience decisions that are difficult because you don't have enough good options to choose from. Take the case of someone who wants to go back to school, but must do so close to home due to family or work obligations. What happens if the only colleges close by aren't particularly strong in the field that person wants to study and the program isn't offered online? The decision becomes one of opting for what's second best or third best, rather than what's ideal. When the choices are no great shakes, the decision is not an easy one to make.

Making matters worse is the fact that so many decisions come with a deadline. If you don't choose X, Y, or Z by such-and-such a date and time, you'll miss out on the chance of a lifetime: a great bargain, your ticket to success, or some other life-changing opportunity. Sometimes, the time deadlines are just come-ons by salespeople or are self-imposed and therefore controllable. Often, however, they are all too real and put such pressure on us that we can't imagine how we'll ever wade through all the choices to get to the right one in time.

Money is an additional factor that can have an impact on decisions. If your financial resources are limited when a purchase or investment is required, then the pressure to make the best decision becomes exacerbated.

YOU'RE NOT ALONE

Procrastinating about consumer purchases is my downfall. I'll shop till I drop before actually buying something as simple as a toaster. I'm as indecisive about clothes. And furniture? Forget it. I've been searching for the perfect sofa-bed for over a year. I know my research obsession is a perfectionist mind game I play with myself, but I just can't seem to break this pattern.

—Jeanne K., publicist

Making Decisions Harder Than They Need to Be

We can't blame all of our decision-making difficulties on external factors, though. Many of us make decisions more difficult than they need to be because of the way we approach them in our minds. We agonize, analyze, deliberate, and debate until what should have been a fairly simple process becomes a torturous ordeal.

Often, perfectionism is the culprit. We feel we can't settle on one option until it is proven to be the perfect choice. Of course, rarely is there one option that's clearly head and shoulders above the others. Waiting for that ideal choice is like searching for sunken treasure. You aren't quite sure if the ideal choice is really out there somewhere, but you hope that it is, and you're willing to go out on a limb to find it. Unfortunately, going out on that limb may keep you from just making a decision with the choices you do have and getting on with your life.

ACTION TACTIC

Think of any big decisions you are currently trying to make. Ask yourself what's holding you back. Then ask yourself if the reasons for delaying are truly valid. Is there another way you could approach the problem in terms of your thought process and emotions around it?

Decisions Strike at the Core of Who We Are

Some decisions raise difficult issues about who we are or who we'd like to be. Take the example of relocating to another city or town as a lifestyle choice (as opposed to going where the jobs are). Any website or book you might turn to on relocation will ask you to rate how important various criteria are to you so that it can tell you which locations match what you're looking for. You have to know, for example, if it's more important for you to be near good hospitals or big universities. Would you rather have cultural attractions and sophisticated nightlife or long bike trails and nice parks? The choices force you to look at what kind of life you lead or would like to lead. No wonder so many people put off finding a place to live. The process requires that you not only look outward at your geographic choices but inward as well.

The same happens with choosing a career, choosing a spouse or life partner, buying a house, or making any other major decision. You have to have a solid handle on who you are as a person before you can know who you want to be with, what you want to do, or where you want to live.

Making Major-League Decisions

What are the decisions that cause you trouble? Some of them belong in the major leagues; they're the ones that can have a serious impact on your life or the lives of people who depend on you. These decisions generally fall into seven categories:

- **Relationships/marriage:** Who to be with; whether to make the commitment; if and when to end it

- **Family decisions:** Decisions related to the care, education, and upbringing of children or about having them in the first place; care of aging parents or other relatives; whether or not to have pets

- **Relocation/home:** Where to live; whether to rent or buy; how much to spend on a rental or purchase; if, when, and how to remodel, renovate, or decorate

- **Career decisions:** Choosing your first career direction or changing an existing one; deciding which types of jobs to seek and evaluating job offers; deciding if and when to start your own business; taking a new role or early retirement offer from your employer; other issues related to developing or managing your career

- **Business decisions:** Any decisions that have to be made in the course of the day on the job or in your own business

- **Financial decisions:** Decisions related to budgeting, spending, and saving; how much, when, and where to invest

- **Personal decisions:** Any decisions related to yourself, including health choices, such as which doctors to see or whether to have certain medical procedures; whether to make changes in your appearance; choices related to your spirituality such as where to worship or whether to change your religious affiliation

QUICKSAND!

Don't waste your time agonizing over too many minor decisions on a day-to-day basis. As often as possible, let someone else (especially when they care more) decide which restaurant to go to, where to hang the new painting for the office lobby, or whether to buy the package with six rolls of toilet paper or eight. Keep your mind clear for the bigger, more critical decisions.

These major-league decisions are the ones that keep us up at night when we're trying to make them and come back to haunt us if we never get around to making them at all.

Making Minor-League Decisions

Our daily lives are filled with micro-decisions, the little decisions we don't even notice we're making but that we usually have to make in order to get anything done. Should you give your child bananas or peaches for breakfast this morning? Will you wear the red tie or the yellow one? At the office, do you answer email or make phone calls first? Most of these are not life-or-death decisions, but they can seem that way for people who find decision-making in general difficult.

Although these decisions may not be as significant as the major-league ones, letting yourself get stressed out over too many little decisions day after day adds up to one big problem. Not only does doing so drain your mental energy (energy you need for more important matters), it keeps your life in a constant state of disarray. By wasting too much time fretting over the small stuff, you're likely to become disorganized and fall behind on more critical tasks in the process.

The Eight Decision-Making Styles

Each of our brains is wired differently when it comes to decision-making. In order to start making better decisions or to stop putting off making them at all, you need to understand your natural decision-making style.

Loner or Pollster?

If you're a loner type, you probably try to make most decisions on your own. It's not your natural inclination to involve others, even if the ultimate decision will affect people around you, such as a spouse or co-worker. You trust your own judgment or feel that the dilemma is not something you should bother people with. If it's a business decision, you don't call a meeting to get input from colleagues. If it's a personal decision, you don't call a family meeting or email all your friends. You go it alone.

Taken to an extreme, the loner position is a handicap, because the input of others is an important element of sound decision-making. On the other hand, a little bit of loner attitude is a practical approach to decision-making; after all is said and done, it's up to you and you alone to decide how you cast your vote.

If you're a pollster type, you do the opposite. You survey anybody and everybody to find out what they know about the options you're choosing among, or you ask them what they would do in your situation. Taken too far, the pollster style can mean that you secretly hope someone else will make the decision for you and will tell you what to do. Used responsibly, though, the pollster method is a good way to make an informed decision. It can also be useful for building consensus when a decision you make will affect the lives or work of others.

Forecaster or Bean-Counter?

Forecasters are, as you might have guessed, future-oriented. They tend to focus on the implications of decisions they're making. They think through where various forks in the road would lead. This visionary approach ensures that a decision you make today won't mess up your life tomorrow, because you've thought through its long-range consequences. A common pitfall of this approach, however, is that you might see the forest but lose sight of the trees; you consider the big picture but overlook critical details.

That's where the bean-counter approach becomes important. Bean-counters focus on the details and the bottom line. They gather the nitty-gritty data that's needed to make a fully informed decision. The key here is to strike a balance between the long-range view of the forecaster and the attention to detail of the bean-counter.

Analyst or Feeler?

I once saw a client in my former career counseling practice who was a 55-year-old engineering professor recently admitted to medical school. He was having an extremely difficult time deciding whether to embark on such a long, arduous route at that point in his life. This man was a perfect example of the analyst style of decision-making. He would come into my office with elaborate spreadsheets and graphs that laid out his options and analyzed the pros and cons of each. Unfortunately, all that fancy data analysis wasn't getting him any closer to a decision. What was missing was the perspective of the feeler.

Good decisions are based on the right balance of head and heart, on analyzing objective data but also listening to what your gut instincts tell you. Feelers listen to what their values tell them is the right thing to do, and they listen to their intuition. Those aren't things that can be plotted on a chart or graph, but they are often just as valid as the analyst's data.

ACTION TACTIC

If you've made bad choices in the past, try to identify where you took the wrong turn in your decision-making process. If you can zero in on what led you to make the wrong choice, you'll be less likely to repeat the same mistake.

Hunter-Gatherer or Settler?

Do you tend to leave no stone unturned when hunting for information to help you make a decision? Do you gather so much information you can't begin to sort through it all? Or do you lose patience with the research process and become so uncomfortable about not having made a decision that you just settle on an option, even if you're not 100 percent sure it's the right one?

As with all of these pairs of decision-making styles, striking the right balance between hunter-gatherer and settler is essential. You have to collect enough information to make an informed decision but not use the research process as an excuse to keep delaying it. You have to call an end to the debating, deliberating, and weighing of options at some point. But you shouldn't make too hasty a decision just for the sake of having one made.

What's Your Decision-Making Style?

You probably see at least a little bit of yourself in each of the eight styles I just described. You may also tend to use one approach with certain types of decisions and the opposite approach with others.

Nevertheless, most everyone has a natural inclination toward one direction or the other, regardless of the type of decision or the setting in which you're making it.

Keep your decision-making styles in mind as you read through the following 10 steps to decision-making. You'll need to pay more or less attention to the various steps depending on your natural tendencies.

Ten Steps to Decision-Making Like a Pro

An easy way to master the art of decision-making is to follow the simple, 10-step process described in the following sections each time you have a difficult choice to make.

1. Assess the importance of the decision. Is this a major- or minor-league decision you're facing? If it's minor, ask yourself how much of your time and mental energy it deserves. Procrastinators often get bogged down in the small stuff. If the matter is fairly trivial, then you should probably just do something and not worry too much about exactly what it is you're doing. Or maybe you can delegate the decision-making to someone else. If it's important, then you need to pay close attention to the steps that follow.

2. Assess your readiness to make a decision. Sometimes, decisions are difficult to make because it's not the right time to be making them. If you have too much going on in your life in the way of major projects, commitments, transitions, or other stressors, then you might not have the time and energy to devote to making a good decision. Many decisions cannot wait, but at least consider where it can.

3. Define your priorities. As with the relocation example given earlier in this chapter, most major decisions require that you define some criteria on which to base the decision.

If you run a small business and need to decide whether to take on a partner, then you need to have your long-term business and personal goals in mind before you can decide if partnership is a good idea.

All sorts of decisions require that we know where we want to end up in the long run before we can feel comfortable deciding what to do today.

QUICKSAND!

All the best decision-making strategies in the world are useless if you don't set aside enough time to make the strategies work. You have to schedule times to conduct research and times to sit back and think about your choices, just as you would schedule an appointment or meeting.

4. Listen to your gut. Before assessing your options in a logical, methodical way, it helps to start by listening to what your gut instincts tell you. (Or listen to your heart, your spirit, or whatever you personally choose to have guide you.) Sometimes, people embark on a long, involved research process to make a decision, only to find that their first instinct had already given them the answer they were looking for. It's usually unwise to base a decision entirely on something as subjective and intangible as a gut feeling, but that's a good place to get your first read.

That engineer considering medical school at midlife finally started listening to his gut as he worked through his decision with my counseling. He began to realize that the recent death of his father made him come face to face with his own mortality and made him feel anxious about achieving his dreams while still alive. He realized that even though he had a genuine interest in being a doctor and had for a very long time, he was now motivated more by an emotional need—a fear of not doing enough or being successful enough.

He'd been hiding his true motivation behind his charts and graphs and hadn't admitted to himself or others that his exploration of med school was something of a knee-jerk emotional reaction. After understanding this, and coupling it with the realization that med school didn't make sense as a good choice "on paper," he decided not to go. But he was glad that he'd at least given it serious thought and could now move on.

5. Gather data. Most good decisions are based on information. You need to talk to people, read about your choices, or do whatever kind of research makes sense for the type of decision you're trying to make. Collect enough data to know what each option entails and how each would affect you and your loved ones personally and professionally.

6. Revisit your criteria. After gathering some information on your options, you might find that your priorities shift a bit. Something you thought was extremely important to you may seem less important now that you know more about the realities of your choices. At this point, it's helpful to go back to Step 3 and reevaluate how critical each of your priorities actually is.

7. Analyze the data. Most people get out the old pad of paper and a pen to make a list of the pros and cons for each option they're considering. And most people still end up unable to make a choice. The problem is that they're often comparing apples and oranges. The best few options out of the bunch usually end up having about the same balance of pros and cons. If they didn't, then you probably wouldn't be faced with a tough choice in the first place; one option would clearly emerge as the best.

The way to get around the apples-and-oranges dilemma is to go back to the priorities you identified in Step 3 and revisited in Step 6. If you know what's most important to you in the area of your life that a particular decision will affect, then you should be able to define some criteria on which to base your decision.

If you're trying to decide between two laptops to buy, for example, your top two criteria might be portability and lowest price for best quality. Out of all your choices, you narrow the options to two. One has a very low price and good reputation, but it seems to weigh a ton. The other one is light and small, but it will hit you harder in the wallet. Do you go with the one that will save you money now but may cost more in the long run because you'll not be able to use it in as many places? Or do you shell out the bigger bucks now and save money in the long run? The only way to make the choice is to know what your priority is. Is your priority to make an investment in your future or is it to get the best equipment you can find now on a limited budget?

ACTION TACTIC

No matter what kind of decision you're trying to make, ranking your decision-making criteria in order of importance is a key to making the tough choices.

8. Listen to your gut—again. Enough with being rational, logical, and methodical; now you need to put aside all that objective data for a moment and listen to what your heart and your gut are telling you to do. Are they still saying the same thing they said before you collected information in Step 5? Or has your instinct changed its tune now that you're better informed about your options?

I'm not saying that you should completely forget about the research you've done and make an impulsive, emotional decision. A good decision is based on both objective and subjective information. At this point in the process, you need to take the tentative decision you've made based on the data analysis in Step 7 and see how that decision sits with you. What looks like the right choice on paper and makes sense in your head may not feel right in your heart.

9. Deal with any roadblocks standing in your way. If you've tried to balance the objective analysis with the subjective approach and are still stuck, try to figure out what's holding you back. When you find yourself unable to make a decision, ask the following questions:

- ❏ Could I benefit from more outside input?
- ❏ Have I done enough research?
- ❏ Do I need to force myself to stop researching and start deciding?
- ❏ Am I trusting my instincts and judgment enough?
- ❏ Am I keeping my priorities and goals in mind?
- ❏ Is fear of making the wrong decision holding me back? Is that fear justified?
- ❏ Am I delaying this decision because I'm concerned about what I'll have to do after I make it?

If you demand honest answers from yourself to all of these questions, you'll zero in on the root of your paralysis, and you'll be able to get past the roadblocks. If you still can't get around the roadblocks on your own, consider working with a coach, career counselor, or psychotherapist for an objective and supportive perspective on the situation.

10. Take the plunge. At some point, you have to do one simple thing: decide already! Keep in mind that most decisions don't come with bells, whistles, and lightbulbs over the head. You might find this tenth step to be somewhat anticlimactic and not exactly an a-ha moment. Don't let that deter you. If you've carefully progressed through the previous nine steps, then you're in a good position to make a sound decision. Go ahead and do it!

Don't Sweat It

Very few decisions in life are totally irreversible. It might be inconvenient, expensive, and even a little embarrassing to admit that you made the wrong choice and need to go back to square one or plan B, but doing so is almost always an option. If you find yourself putting too much pressure on any decision you make, keep in mind that having freedom of choice is supposed to be a good thing; it shouldn't be something that causes undue stress.

The Least You Need to Know

- When you delay making decisions, you put your life on hold and miss out on opportunities.
- Decision-making is a skill that can be learned.
- We often make decisions more difficult than they need to be because we expect the perfect choice to materialize before us.
- Avoid spending too much time on minor decisions, and instead save your time and energy for the bigger ones.
- Good decisions are based on a combination of rational analysis and listening to your gut instincts.
- When faced with difficult decisions, follow the simple 10-step method described in this chapter.

The Prescription for Overcoming Procrastination

In This Chapter

- Three simple steps to stop procrastination in its tracks
- How to use the stop, look, and listen solution to break the procrastination habit
- Ten techniques for getting anything done

I wish I could tell you that the prescription for overcoming procrastination is something as easy as popping a pill. It's not quite that simple, but I *can* tell you it's not too difficult, either. The key is to use a behavioral and mental approach that addresses the external and internal causes of procrastination in order to stop it before it kicks in. This approach is the "stop, look, and listen" solution described in this chapter.

Then, to take action and get things done, have a repertoire of simple tips and tricks on hand as described in the "Ten Surefire Strategies for Getting Anything Done" section of this chapter.

The Stop, Look, and Listen Solution

When you were a child, your parents or teachers might have taught you to cross the street safely by warning you to do three things: stop, look, and listen. That same advice works when you feel a bout of procrastination coming on. You know from Chapters 2 and 3 that procrastination creeps into your life and stalls you out because some combination of environmental and psychological factors is at work. The stop, look, and listen solution addresses all of these factors by having you examine what's going on around you and in your head so that you can counteract the causes of procrastination before it takes over. The following sections examine each element of this technique and show you how to make it work for you.

Just Push Pause—Using the "Stop" Part of the Solution

It's a lazy Sunday afternoon. The Packers or Saints or Steelers (or your team of choice) have just called a time-out, so you go into the kitchen to make a sandwich. After you finish, you leave the open bag of bread, a messy mustard knife, and lots of crumbs on the counter and head back to the television. Somewhere in that process, the fleeting thought "I'll clean it up later" runs through your mind. After all, it's first and goal, so you really need to get back to the game—never mind that the sandwich took barely a minute to make so there's actually time for a quick clean-up before play resumes.

Leaving a few crumbs and a knife that will get crusty is probably not going to wreck your life, but it may be just one example of many instances of procrastination that do start to take their toll on your quality of life and the people around you. To break the pattern of putting things off until some vague future time, the first thing to do is, surprisingly, not to take action but to stop. Stop to think about what you're doing and try to figure out why you're doing it.

ACTION TACTIC

Imagine you're watching a videotape of yourself and you push the pause button. Picture yourself on the screen, frozen in time. That's what I want you to do in real life. Every time you're walking away from your desk to avoid doing work, slinking out of a room that needs cleaning, or avoiding any other task, push an imaginary pause button and freeze your movement.

When you say "Stop!" to yourself, you do several important things:

- You are no longer acting on impulse; you instead become conscious of your behavior.

- You gain power over procrastination instead of letting it be some insidious force that sneaks up on you.

- You give yourself the chance to think about the consequences of delaying the task you're about to put off.

- You give yourself the chance to get angry or fed up over your procrastination habit, and these emotions may inspire you to do something about it.

If you end up still deciding to put off the task, it's okay as long as that decision is based on pausing to think about what you're doing. You might decide, for example, that Sundays are meant for relaxing and that you really don't want to take a chance of missing any of the game, so there's nothing wrong with waiting until later (half-time, maybe?) to clean up the kitchen. That's fine, as long as you've stopped to think about what you're doing and aren't merely acting on impulse.

Think of this step in the technique as being like pushing the pause button on a remote control. The second you sense that a procrastination moment is about to arise, hit the pause button. Yes, you have to conjure up some sheer willpower and self-discipline at first to make this happen, but after you do it a while, it will become second nature. I've been using this technique for years, and believe me, considering how challenged I am in the willpower and self-discipline arenas, if I can do it, I know anyone can.

Look Around You—Using the "Look" Part of the Solution

When you've called a halt to that first impulse to procrastinate, the next step is to look around for the reasons you're tempted to put something off. You're basically looking for five types of problems, much like those described in Chapter 2.

- Is clutter getting in your way?

- Is something distracting you?

- Is someone distracting you?

- Are you uncomfortable?

- Do you not have enough, or the correct, information, tools, or supplies to get the task done?

After you've pushed the pause button on that imaginary video of yourself, imagine you're examining what you see on the screen as though you were looking for a movie prop that was out of place or something else you couldn't catch when the video was playing. Do the same in real life. Literally look around for distractions or missing information that's keeping you from taking action.

Can't put the dirty mustard knife away because the dishwasher's full of clean dishes? Make a pact with yourself to empty the dishwasher during half-time so you can put away the darn knife. Or just rinse it off by hand!

When you've identified what's getting in your way, think about what you can do to remove the roadblocks. Take some time to clear out and organize the clutter, remove the distractions, get comfortable, or find the information and guidance you need.

YOU'RE NOT ALONE

My sister and I once won a free pair of snow skis. We couldn't decide which length would be better for us in terms of our level of experience and the amount we ski. It's now been two years, and my sister still hasn't called to claim the skis. I imagine it's now too late to get them.

—Rebecca R., graduate student

Listen Carefully—Using the "Listen" Part of the Solution

The next step is to listen to what's going on in your head. As described in Chapter 3, your thoughts, feelings, and internal messages (self-talk) drive your actions. To put an end to those games your mind plays, ask yourself these three sets of questions and listen closely to the answers:

1. What am I feeling? Am I giving in to fear or negative feelings about the task that lies before me or about my ability to do it? Am I feeling overwhelmed when it's not necessary to feel that way? Am I feeling pressured to get this done by a certain time or in a certain way? Am I bored or tired?

2. What am I thinking? Are my thoughts irrational, unreasonable, inaccurate, or self-sabotaging? Am I assuming this task is going to be more difficult or unpleasant than it is likely to be? Am I believing that I don't have enough time to do this? Is that true? Am I convincing myself that X has to happen before I can do Y? Am I justified in waiting for X?

3. What am I saying to myself (or out loud to others)? Are negative or unproductive statements running through my mind? Am I giving myself permission to put this off or making excuses? Am I saying things that I haven't even been conscious of and that are powerful barriers to action? For example, am I saying things such as: "I don't have to do this now; I'll do that later; I'm just not the sort of person who does that"?

By asking these questions, you break down your internal barriers to action. You stop functioning on autopilot and start becoming conscious of the thoughts, feelings, and self-talk behind your acts of procrastination. Later in this chapter, in "Strategy 7: Use Positive Self-Talk," you'll learn techniques for replacing these paralyzing thoughts, feelings, and statements with more positive ones.

 YOU'RE NOT ALONE

I generally avoid temptation unless I can't resist it.

—Mae West, actress

Ten Surefire Strategies for Getting Anything Done

The stop, look, and listen formula squashes the impulse to procrastinate and forces you to deal head-on with the reasons you're about to put off something. What it doesn't do, however, is get the thing done. That's where the 10 strategies that follow come in. Think of them as a bag of tricks you can pull from when you find yourself about to put off starting something or not finishing what you've started.

The 10 strategies don't have to be used in the order in which they're listed here. This is not a 10-step process in which you have to do Strategy 1, then 2, and so on. Instead, use whichever one works for the situation you find yourself in. If you're facing a tough procrastination situation, you might have to try several strategies before you get to the one that motivates you to take action. The idea is to pick and choose until you get to the one that works for you.

Strategy 1: Get Fired Up

This strategy involves doing a reality check. Depending on the situation, that might mean getting really fed up with yourself, really embarrassed by your behavior, or really angry that other people are leaving you in their dust while you procrastinate. Procrastinators often float through life in a state of denial, believing that there's not much harm in what they're doing (or not doing). Or even worse, they don't think about their behavior at all, much less whether it's doing any harm. The idea behind this strategy is that it's not just a reality check: it's a wake-up call. By getting fired up, you think through the potential negative consequences that can result from putting off something or that have resulted in the past when you procrastinated about something comparable. The emotions that result when you get fired up can spark some powerful action.

ACTION TACTIC

Designate one day a month, or whatever works for your schedule, as a "Stop-the-World-I-Wanna-Get-Off" day. On this day, you don't have to take care of any of your usual chores or responsibilities. You use the entire day to catch up on busy work or a time-consuming project, get reorganized, or in some other way regroup and reconnect.

Strategy 2: Get Organized

As you already know from Chapters 5 and 6, getting rid of clutter and unnecessary obligations and becoming organized are important foundations to productivity. They were presented as ways of cleaning out your life to clear the way for taking action, sort of prerequisites for becoming an ex-procrastinator. Now you can use those same strategies when you're on the brink of procrastinating.

If you're in the middle of a project and find yourself losing steam, look around to see if clutter has accumulated since you first began. If so, is it making you feel unmotivated to do any more or making your job harder than it ought to be? If you haven't even started on something yet, the same principle applies. If you're faced with clutter and chaos or a life that's on overload, you're going to be reluctant to tackle the task that lies within the mess. Taking a little time to get organized clears the way for being productive.

Strategy 3: Prioritize

You can't get things done unless you make it a priority to do them. I realize that sounds so obvious that it hardly seems worth mentioning, but most people don't prioritize effectively, so it needs to be said. It's easy to go through daily life in your usual routine saying, "I wish I could get X done because it's a priority to me, but I just can't seem to find the time for it." Or even worse, you might say, "I wish I could get X done, but it just isn't happening." Things don't just happen by themselves, and a few extra hours per day aren't going to miraculously appear. You have to rearrange the way you're choosing to spend the 24 hours a day you are given.

ACTION TACTIC

If you organize a schedule for getting routine tasks done, it clears your mind to think about more interesting things.

Strategy 4: Find Freedom in Routine

Having a schedule that determines the days and/or times when you'll do recurring tasks and chores is routine but not constricting. You can vary your routine as the need arises or when you don't feel like doing something at its designated time. You control your routine; it doesn't control you.

A routine is liberating in that it keeps you from worrying about what you should be, ought to be, or could be doing. Some people shun the idea of a routine because they think it will make their life dull and not give them the freedom to be spontaneous or creative. The irony is that the things you need to schedule into a weekly routine are usually pretty dull in the first place, so you're not missing out on anything by working them into a routine. When you designate days and/or times to do these mundane tasks, you don't have to worry about them the rest of the time. On a Monday, I can walk guilt free past a laundry basket that's getting pretty full because I know I always do laundry on Tuesdays.

Strategy 5: Get Comfortable

One of the simplest ways to get motivated to do something is to get more comfortable. When I'm in the middle of writing a chapter or an article and find myself stuck, unable to write any more, the technique that often works is to print out what I've written so far, get out of my desk chair, and curl up on the sofa in another room with my printout, a pen, and a pad of paper. I find that getting my hands off the keyboard, changing my position, and gaining a fresh perspective on my writing from the hard copy rather than the screen does wonders for getting past writer's block. (Yes, it is possible to move to the couch without falling asleep—sometimes.)

Strategy 6: Get Connected to People and Information

Isolation is the kiss of death to action. You have to reach out to people and to sources of information to find the guidance, new ideas, support, and companionship that enable you to stop stalling and get moving. I don't mean that you're going to do your best work on a crowded city bus or in the middle of an amusement park. Working alone or in a quiet environment is a great way to get things done. What I do mean is that there's a difference between working independently and being isolated.

The danger of isolation is that you become disconnected from people and from information that could help you do your work better, faster, or more easily. You can easily become a hermit if you do your job from home, do housework alone, or try to tackle any personal, self-improvement issues on your own. Even if you work in a large company, it's easy to close that office door (or hole up in your cubicle) and disconnect yourself from the people around you.

Strategy 7: Use Positive Self-Talk

As I've discussed in previous chapters, the messages that play in your head have a great deal of power over your behavior. When you give in to negative emotions, irrational thoughts, and destructive self-talk, you open the floodgates to procrastination. An important strategy that works for just about every procrastination situation is to play more positive messages in your head.

You start by substituting positive thoughts for negative ones, then you learn to speak a new internal language to make your self-talk more likely to lead to action.

Old Speak	New Speak
I don't think I can do that.	I know it seems difficult now, but I can get it done.
I can't get that done on time.	If I make this a priority, I can get it done on time.
I'm not the kind of person who does X.	I used to be a procrastinator, but now I'm the type of person who gets X done.
I'm afraid I won't do this well enough.	It doesn't have to be perfect; it just has to get done.

continues

continued

I should do that even though I already have enough to do.	Do I really have to do that? If not, I don't need to feel guilty for not doing it.
I can't see myself doing that.	I can visualize myself starting and finishing it as if I were watching myself in a video.
I would do that, but …	I will do that because …

Those are several of the most common examples of negative self-talk. The key is to eliminate the negative language—words such as *not*, *afraid*, and *but*—and also to be creative in thinking about the flip side of the negative thought behind that language.

Strategy 8: Focus on Do Dates, not Due Dates

In a way, deadlines are meaningless. The date that something is due is simply the date that you turn it in, hand it over, mail or email it, present it, or stop working on it. Whether it's a deadline at work, a deadline to apply for something, or a deadline you've set for yourself in your personal life, that deadline or due date has almost nothing to do with action.

A major reason why people put off things and end up racing to meet a deadline is that they focus too much on the due date and not enough on do dates. Do dates are the specific days or times when you schedule and plan to complete certain tasks. Do dates are where the action is.

MATTER OF FACT

The word *deadline* stems from the dead line during the Civil War, which was a line drawn in the dirt around prison camps or stockades. If a prisoner crossed the line, guards were authorized to shoot him dead on the spot with no warning. Thus, we have the term *deadline*, which still causes as much anxiety today as it did then, even when the circumstances aren't life or death!

Many experts in productivity and project management suggest setting mini-deadlines that come before the final deadline. The mini-deadlines give you something more manageable and less remote to work toward. This system is still not enough for a true procrastinator, though. You just end up with more deadlines to race toward or miss. Although there's no harm in using the mini-deadline system, it won't work unless you also schedule do dates that will lead you to meeting those deadlines.

Strategy 9: Use the Chip-Away Technique

The chip-away strategy involves tackling big projects or working toward major goals by chipping away at them with little bits of action here and there. If your goal is to get in better physical shape, you might find five minutes to do some exercises at your desk when you can't tear yourself away for an hour at the gym. If you're trying to write a term paper for school but can't seem to get started, you could take two minutes to skim through a relevant article while you're waiting for class to start. Some ideas in that article might inspire you to get cracking on the paper. If you've been putting off weeding the garden and find yourself standing in the driveway waiting for your spouse or the kids to come out to the car, reach down to pull up a few weeds from the front path.

Even though it's extremely important to schedule times when you'll do routine tasks or take steps in major projects, it's just as important that you be on the lookout for unexpected windows of opportunity. Using this hidden time, time when you aren't necessarily scheduled to work on a particular task, is a great way to chip away at that task.

ACTION TACTIC

For more ideas on how to chip away at your goals and projects, refer to *Stop Screaming at the Microwave: How to Connect Your Disconnected Life,* in which Mary LoVerde describes a concept similar to the chip-away technique, which she calls "microactions."

Strategy 10: Play Trick or Treat

Just as the procrastination habit can sneak up on you, you can sneak up on it with tricks and treats that motivate you to take action:

- **Distract yourself.** You might feel that in order to get things done, you have to turn off the television or phone, shut down the video games, stay away from the shopping mall, keep your chatty friends and co-workers at bay, or avoid any other so-called timewaster or distraction that limits your productivity. The fact is, though, when you deprive yourself of something you enjoy or put yourself in an artificially sterile environment, you are often less productive.

  I'm not saying you should try to write your Great American Novel while engrossed in an action-suspense thriller on television, but putting a small television in the kitchen might make you more likely to scrub those pots and pans or even to cook. The idea is to look for ways to combine doing what you enjoy with doing what you don't necessarily like to do but need to do.

- **Dangle a carrot.** There's nothing like the promise of a reward for a job well done to get you motivated. Delayed gratification doesn't work for everybody, but looking forward to a treat you've promised yourself is a handy technique to try. Plus, it helps ensure that you're keeping some balance of work and fun in your life.

- **Beat the clock.** Pretend that you have a limited period of time in which to get something done and see how fast you can do it. Suppose you're trying to clean out the garage. You estimate that you have about three hours of work left to do, but you don't feel like working for three more minutes, much less three more hours. Pretend that you have only one hour left before someone will be coming over to see the finished product. Play a game of seeing how much you can finish in that hour. You might be surprised to find that you get three hours' worth of work done in an hour because of the imaginary time limit. But even if you don't, you've at least done more than if you had given up altogether.

- **Pretend you're about to go on vacation.** You may know the feeling of going on vacation from a full-time job or a business you run. In the last few days, or even the last few hours, before that vacation, you probably get more work done than in a typical week on the job. The necessity of getting projects wrapped up or loose ends taken care of provides an adrenaline rush that propels your action into warp speed. (Plus, it helps to know that there's a light at the end of the tunnel in the form of white, sandy beaches or wherever it is that you're headed.)

  You may not be able to go on an actual vacation, but you can play a trick on yourself based on that pre-vacation productivity boost. The game may encourage you to take stock of what you've fallen behind on and get it done or to move forward with something you've been putting off starting.

- **Just do something.** I'm no physicist, but I believe physicists when they say that an object at rest will remain at rest until some force propels it into motion. It's a handy principle to keep in mind when trying to get yourself to do something. Sometimes nothing works better than to take one little baby step toward a particular task. You'll more than likely find that the first step propels you into motion and leads to more steps. If I reach into a dishwasher of clean dishes to take out the one bowl I need, I often find that I say to myself, "Well, I might as well go ahead and empty the whole machine."

The act of procrastinating involves all sorts of mind games we play on ourselves. By playing trick or treat, we can turn those mind games to our advantage.

MATTER OF FACT

The "just do something" strategy and the chip-away technique may sound like the same thing, but they're not. The chip-away technique is based on making use of down time or hidden time to do anything at all related to a bigger task, even if what you do is not necessarily the first step. The "just do something" strategy is all about taking the first step toward a task in the hope that that step will propel you into the next step. It's a subtle difference, but a difference nevertheless.

See? It's Not So Hard!

If you feel an invasion of the procrastination body-snatchers headed toward you, you now know what to do. First, you stop, look, and listen to break the pattern of acting on impulse and to figure out what's keeping you from taking action. Then, you choose from the 10 strategies for getting things done until you find the one that works for you and for the situation you're stuck in.

The Least You Need to Know

- When you feel yourself starting to put off something, use the prescription for halting procrastination in its tracks: stop, look, and listen.
- Procrastination is a habit based on impulsive action, so stopping, or pausing, to think about what you're doing and the consequences of delaying is the first step toward breaking the habit.
- When you're tempted to put off something, look around you to see what's tripping you up, such as distractions or clutter in your environment or something that's making you uncomfortable.
- Listening to your thoughts, feelings, and self-talk is critical for understanding why you're about to start procrastinating.
- When you just can't seem to get yourself to take action, refer to the list of 10 strategies to get moving, and pick the ones that work for you and for the type of task you're putting off.

Let's Get It Done (Already)

In Part 2, you laid the foundation for becoming an ex-procrastinator by getting your act together through decluttering, organizing, and better decision-making and by learning how to manage your actions with the stop, look, and listen solution and the 10 tips. Part 3 focuses on more nitty-gritty techniques for getting things done in particular areas of your life. Whether you're determined to lose weight, find a mate, or stop being late, these chapters are for you.

In Chapter 9, you'll find tips for overcoming procrastination at home, whether you need to wash that sink full of dishes or change the smoke alarm batteries. Chapter 10 focuses on making things happen in your family and social life, then Chapter 11 moves into realities of life such as making an overdue doctor's appointment, keeping New Year's resolutions, or putting together a will.

In Chapter 12, you'll learn how to get ahead in life—and be happy while you do it—at work or school. And whether you work, go to school, or keep the home fires burning, Chapter 13 will help you be more efficient with, rather than bogged down by, technology.

The book closes with Chapter 14, in which you'll see how you really can make procrastination a closed chapter in your life and get things done without sacrificing mind, body, or soul.

Let's Get It Done (Already)

Part 5

Procrastination in Your Home Life

In This Chapter

- Why you hate housework
- (Almost) effortless tidying and cleaning
- Laundry, trash, and other drudgery
- Tool time
- Yucky yard work

Have you ever come across those people who enjoy household chores? The ones who find it relaxing to iron or invigorating to vacuum and who consider mowing the lawn a Zenlike experience? If you're reading this chapter, you're probably not part of that rare breed. Don't worry; I'm not going to try to sell you on the joys of housework. I merely want to help you understand why you put off projects around the house and offer tips for getting them taken care of relatively painlessly. Because let's face it: They have to get done somehow by somebody, and lots of times the only somebody is you.

Are You a Neatnik, Clean Freak, or Slob?

Do you align the edges of magazines on the coffee table while ignoring the tumbleweeds of dust under the table? Do you neatly put away dishes and clear off countertops in the kitchen every night but never mop the floor until your feet stick to it? If so, you're like me: a neat-nik who can go an embarrassingly long time without vacuuming (I'm satisfied just to pick up the big pieces of debris by hand), but who can't stand to see sofa cushions that need fluffing and throw pillows out of kilter.

YOU'RE NOT ALONE

You know things are bad when you've got five minutes before company arrives and have to make decisions like, "Do I put on my makeup and get dressed, or do I vacuum?" Makeup and clothes always win hands-down, and the dust gets swept under the couch.

—Barbara W., business manager

Or maybe you're like the husband of a friend of mine. She tells him that company is coming over in 20 minutes and asks him to help her tidy up the house. He says, "Don't you worry about it. I'll take care of it." Nineteen minutes later, she finds that he's taken apart the toaster to render it impeccably crumb free, scrubbed the bathtub (which the guests won't even see, much less be using), and vacuumed every nook and cranny of the carpets and floorboards. If he'd had an hour before guests were to arrive, he would also have rewired a lamp or two and repotted some houseplants.

What he doesn't do during those critical minutes is pick up and put away the toys, clothes, papers, magazines, books, and other assorted items strewn across every surface of their house. When we arrive at the friend's house, we invariably find her frantically clearing a path from the front door to the couch so we can sit somewhere. But my, isn't the carpet clean! Her husband can't help it; he's a clean freak, through and through.

Then, of course, there are those poor souls who don't care much for either tidying up or cleaning up. Those of us who fall in one of the other two categories think of them as slobs. Chances are they aren't slobs by nature, and they don't enjoy living in squalor; they just can't seem to find the time or energy to maintain their households. They procrastinate. Whichever label rings a bell: neatnik, clean freak, or slob, or a little of each, this chapter has something for you.

Why We Put Off Household Chores

The roots of procrastination on the home front are pretty obvious. Household chores are boring, messy, and sometimes strenuous. Often, we avoid them simply because we have no interest in them. Or we feel too tired after work, school, or parenting to get down on our hands and knees and scrub the bathtub or lug heavy bags of trash out the door. However, three additional factors that are involved in putting off household chores may not be so obvious:

1. You don't have the right cleaning supplies or equipment; you have too many cleaning supplies; or the ones you have are not easily accessible.

2. There are too many other demands on your time, so housework gets relegated to the bottom of your priority list.

3. Your family, friends, or roommates have unrealistic standards for how you should maintain your home. Or you feel pressured by the standards of society at large for housekeeping (made worse by the glistening kitchen floors and toilet bowls in cleaning product advertisements). You feel like you can't live up to everyone's demands, so you waste your time worrying instead of doing.

Recognizing the role that these factors play in household procrastination can get you three steps closer to getting your chores done. You may not ever come to love doing housework (or yard work or washing the car), but you can use some simple techniques to solve these supply and demand problems and stop putting off tasks at home.

Turn Home Squalid Home into Home Sweet Home

The holy trinity of household chores has to be tidying up, cleaning up, and cleaning out. By tidying up, I mean collecting all the random items that end up scattered around the house while you're busy living in it and putting them in their places. Cleaning up is that thing some people do to keep germs, dust, mildew, mold, bugs, and even rodents at bay. Cleaning out is, essentially, decluttering. The following sections look at ways to stop putting off any aspect of these three categories of chores.

ACTION TACTIC

If you tend to sit around a messy house watching television, use the chip-away technique to get things done during commercials. Get up off your duff and pick up a couple of things, load the dishwasher, or wash a few dishes. After a couple of hours of watching television, you might be pleasantly surprised to find that you've made a big dent in your household chores.

To keep your home neat and tidy, follow these six rules:

1. Declutter. It is infinitely easier to straighten up when you have less stuff.

2. Have places to put stuff. If you have a hook to hang your house keys on (or a bowl to drop them in) every time you step in your door, then you know how simple it is to put them away and find them the next time you're headed out. Your goal should be to have that sort of system for everything in your home. Many people put off tidying up because there's no place to put things.

3. Use collection bins. You can chip away at tidying up throughout the day when you keep a basket, box, or other portable container in each room. Suppose that over the weekend, your entrance hall tends to accumulate items of clothing, shoes, papers, sports equipment, books, and anything else that gets dropped there as people come and go. If you have some sort of collection bin that everything can be dropped into and that you can easily carry around to other rooms, you'll be more likely to put everything away.

4. Never walk through your house empty-handed. Get into the habit of taking something with you every time you go from one room to another. For example, at night I sometimes read things in bed that belong in my home office. It's easy for

those items to accumulate in the bedroom unless I make a point of carrying at least one or two of them out with me the next morning.

5. Play beat the clock. Most of us are familiar with having to race against the clock to tidy up when guests are coming over or a client is visiting our office. What we usually don't do, however, is play beat the clock when no one is expected. If you have a competitive streak, you might find that you get motivated to tidy up if you time yourself and see how quickly you can get one room, or even several rooms, or your office, picked up.

6. Focus on one room at a time. One of the biggest mistakes people make when tidying up is to try to work on more than one room at a time. For example, a father of small children uses his collection bin in the den to carry toys to the kids' room. When he gets to that room, he puts all the toys away where they belong and then decides to start straightening up that room or finds some distraction that keeps him there for a while. He ends up forgetting about the tidying up he was doing in the den and may never get back to it. What he should've done instead was drop the toys in the kids' room and quickly get back to the den to finish his job there. By concentrating on one room at a time, you just about guarantee that you'll get at least one area of your home in good shape. Your sense of accomplishment when you see one room looking nice can also encourage you to move on to other rooms.

ACTION TACTIC

When focusing on getting your house in order, don't forget about home safety. If you've been lax about security or fire prevention, schedule firm appointments with yourself (and any experts you need to involve) to establish or refresh burglar and fire safety measures in your home. Also, make sure that all members of the household know where to find fire extinguishers, how to keep your home fully locked up and secure, and who is responsible for changing smoke alarm batteries and on which dates.

Once you have a system in place for getting and keeping your home neat and tidy, you do eventually have to clean it. People who know me well know I'm about the last person on Earth to be qualified to offer cleaning tips. Beyond knowing that club soda can slurp up a red wine stain and that vinegar isn't just for salad dressings but can actually clean things, I'm no Heloise. I do, however, know a lot about the psychology of cleaning, and when it comes to procrastinating about cleaning, that's what we're dealing with.

One way to motivate yourself to clean is to eliminate the number of steps involved (such as having to drag the vacuum cleaner out of a crowded closet and up the stairs to vacuum the second floor of a house). When you minimize the number of steps you have to take to find cleaning supplies or equipment (by forking over the bucks to buy a second vacuum cleaner to keep on the second floor, for example), you give yourself fewer chances to say, "This is too much trouble; I'll do it later." You also have to minimize the thought that goes into cleaning by having a routine for it so that it becomes a habit instead of something you worry about but don't take action on.

ACTION TACTIC

If your home is in bad shape, plan a party so that you'll have to straighten up and clean. Just make sure the party date is far enough in the future to allow you time to whip the house into shape!

Try these additional tips and tricks to move yourself from thinking that you ought to be cleaning to actually cleaning:

- Get someone else to do it! If you hate to clean, or have other ways you need to be spending your time, then this is the obvious answer. If you think you can't afford to hire someone to clean your house, make sure that's really the case. Maybe you could have someone come once every two weeks or have a cleaning service come in once a month to do the heavy-duty chores. Perhaps a neighborhood kid would like to earn a few bucks by coming in to do nothing but vacuum or mop the kitchen and bathroom floors or do any other single chore that you dread doing. Be resourceful.

- Have a daily, weekly, and periodic cleaning routine. Whether you're doing it yourself or have brought in a cleaning whiz, having a routine takes the worry out of cleaning. Start by making a list of everything that needs to be done, and then assign days and times to do it all.

- Get your supplies in order. Weed out the ones that don't work well, are too complicated to use, or have expired. Keep just a few basic, multipurpose cleansers on hand (such as ones that clean both glass and surfaces, or both kitchen and bathroom) so that you don't have to fish through lots of clutter to get to them.

- Use supplies that do most of the work. As you select those few basic cleansers to have on hand, look for ones that let you be a little lazy. For example, you can spritz certain cleansers on the tile after showering, and grime and mildew magically disappear without scrubbing.

- Do it without even realizing you're doing it. If you wait for a big block of time to clean, you'll start to dread all the chores that face you and will be more likely to put it off. Instead, try to clean little by little. If you're cooking, for example, and find that you're waiting for water to boil before you can do anything else, why not grab a hand-vacuum and suck up the crumbs that have accumulated around the toaster or bread box? Or you could wipe off a shelf in the refrigerator.

- Combine cleaning with something fun. Put on your favorite music or let yourself watch something totally useless but amusing on television. Do anything that will make cleaning less of a chore.

MATTER OF FACT

When did you last dust the tops of tall bookcases, clean out the gutters, and disinfect your trash cans? Don't remember? Then you probably need to make lists of cleaning chores you should be doing on a daily, weekly, monthly, and seasonal basis, and schedule those chores into your planner and calendar. The lists can also help you see which chores should be part of your regular routine and which could be delegated to a cleaning service you bring in periodically.

No matter which tricks and techniques work for you, one of the most important strategies is not to stress out over keeping your home perfectly clean. Do what is necessary to make it a comfortable, safe environment (germs are no laughing matter, so I'm not saying don't clean at all), but don't set impossibly high standards that make your life miserable.

> **YOU'RE NOT ALONE**
>
> Believe it or not, I've been carrying 200 unopened boxes with me from apartment to apartment for the past five years. I've had to move three times during my four years in my current city. Unpacking only to pack again seems like a fruitless endeavor, so I just let the boxes sit and wait.
>
> —Dianne D., communications coordinator

Dealing with Laundry, Trash, and Other Dirty Words

Do you know why it's so easy to let trash and dirty clothes pile up? It's because they can be tucked away out of sight. Unlike the layers of dust that are so visible on furniture and the coats of grime that make bathrooms disgusting, garbage is hidden away in cans or bags, and laundry is in a hamper or closet. Yes, I know that the trash can often get pretty darn visible when it overflows and becomes smelly, and dirty clothes might spill out of the closet or hamper. But they are still easier to put out of sight and, therefore, out of mind. Let's look at why you might put off doing laundry, having dry cleaning done, or taking out the trash, and what you can do about it.

Laundry

Do you buy new underwear more often than you do laundry? If so, you're a laundry procrastinator. I used to be one, too. When I moved to New York City after graduate school, one of my first apartments was a fifth-floor walk-up in an old brownstone. It was charming with its exposed brick wall and working fireplace, but charm didn't get the clothes washed. To do that, I had to load up the laundry bag, drag it down 10 flights of stairs (2 per floor), and schlep it down the street three blocks to a laundromat. Then, of course, there was the fun of sitting there for hours watching the dryer spin around, because I didn't dare leave my precious cargo unattended.

After a couple of months, I'd had enough of that and decided to splurge on having my laundry done for me. For about the cost of a movie ticket, I was able to drop off my laundry on the way to work in the morning and pick it up all fresh and neatly folded on my way home. Sure, I still had to get it there, but I made that a no-brainer by taking it on the same day every week so that it became a habit. Knowing that I wouldn't have to wash and dry the clothes myself gave me lots more incentive to drag it down those steps.

Whether you have to haul your dirty duds to a laundromat or just down the basement stairs to your own washer and dryer, think of strategies that will work for your own laundry procrastination. Maybe it's delegating the task to a roommate or family member with the promise that you'll take over one of their chores. Don't think you're the only person in the household capable of doing laundry; teach someone how to do it. It's not rocket science.

If delegating or sending it out isn't an option, look for other ways to get it done. Have a routine for it so that you don't have to worry about it all the time. Make sure your laundry area is clean and uncluttered. If space allows, use those nifty laundry bags or hampers that are divided into two or three sections so that you can sort your dirty clothes by color or water temperature, rather than having to do it just before you wash them. As added incentive, think about how much nicer it is to have clean underwear and towels.

 YOU'RE NOT ALONE

I never do laundry in any week with a Monday.

—Barbara Walters on *The View,* March 26, 1999

Dry Cleaning

Twenty-five percent of the people who took the procrastination survey said that dropping off or picking up dry cleaning is something they procrastinate about, but only 15 percent put off doing laundry. At first glance, those results seem surprising because laundry is typically a bigger, more time-consuming job than tossing a few shirts on the dry cleaner's counter and picking them up all pressed and starched a couple of days later.

But when you think about it, dry cleaning is a multistep process that offers lots of opportunity for procrastination. First, you have to get the clothes out the door, because they can't walk to the cleaner's on their own. To make that happen, keep a shopping bag or tote bag—or one of those sacks the cleaners give you—hanging on your bedroom or closet door to drop your dry cleaning into so that it's always ready to grab at a moment's notice.

Then, unless your dry cleaner picks up and delivers, make sure you take the clothes to a cleaner that's convenient (on your way to work, your kids' school, or your usual errands). Some cleaners even have drive-thru windows to make the process easier.

Next, you have to keep track of the receipt. Find one place in your wallet, purse, car, or wherever and always put receipts there. Just make sure that you'll always have them with you when you need to pick up the clothes. To get the clothes picked up, try to have a standard day(s) of the week (or month, if you have dry cleaning less frequently) that you drop them off and pick them up. As with any other task, having a routine makes it a habit instead of a chore.

Trash

Hearing family members and roommates nag each other about not taking out the trash (and recyclables) often enough or promptly enough is part of the fabric of American culture and probably many other countries' cultures as well. Why is it such a big deal? Like many household chores, it's a dirty, sometimes heavy job that nobody likes to do. Some of the excuses that otherwise hygienic, conscientious people give for letting their trash pile up include the following:

> "The trash can (or trash chute, if in a building) is out of my way."

> **Excuse buster:** If it's not on your way, make it on your way. Work it into your daily routine so that you don't have to make a big deal out of doing it. If you don't already pass the trash cans or chute on your way to your car or walking out to work, vary your route every other day (or however often you need to take out the trash) so that you do pass them. Don't give in to laziness! The trash cans or chute can't be that far away.

> "I don't have time to take the trash out. I'll be late for work/school/whatever."

> **Excuse buster:** Stop the problem before it happens by not letting yourself get so pressed for time. When you're calculating how much time you need between waking up and walking out the door, you factor in things like brushing your teeth, getting dressed, making coffee, wolfing down some breakfast, and scanning the news. Added to that time should be a couple of minutes for bagging up the trash and walking down the hall, out back, down the driveway, or wherever to dump it.

> "I have too many other things to carry when I leave the house."

> **Excuse buster:** First of all, do you have to carry so much stuff? Sometimes, people are not only packrats at home but also when they go places. Try to take less stuff or consolidate what you must take into fewer bags. If you collect your trash in large bags, try switching to smaller bags, such as plastic grocery bags with handles. They'll be easier to carry when you don't have a free hand, just a couple of free fingers.

"The bags always break by the time I get to the trash receptacle, so I dread doing it."

Excuse buster: Buy stronger bags and don't cram so much trash into them. This excuse is really lame (but one that I've used myself, so I know how tempting it is!).

Most of these excuses are just plain old habit. When you stop to think about them (using the stop, look, and listen solution described in Chapter 8), you'll realize that they aren't particularly valid excuses at all.

This Old House

In the procrastination survey, making home repairs or arranging for others to do them was one of the tasks respondents most often cited as being a problem for them. Much of the reason for this may be that having something break, leak, squeak, or otherwise get out of whack is not at all part of one's daily routine. We drop off dry cleaning on Monday mornings and pick it up on Thursdays. We vacuum on Saturdays and cut the grass on Sunday afternoon. What we don't have as part of our routine is fixing a closet door that suddenly doesn't close right or finding a plumber to repair a leaky faucet and rearranging our schedules to be home while the work is being done. To keep the roof over your head not only standing, but functioning well, try these tricks:

- Keep a running list of nonurgent repairs to be done and schedule times to do them, just as you would schedule any other appointments or chores. In addition to doing them at scheduled times, you can also do them whenever you have some down time. Having the list helps you get a quick glimpse at what needs to be done so that when you have a few minutes free and are feeling motivated to do something, you won't have to try to remember what needs fixing. You'll see it on the list.

- Also keep a running list of supplies or tools needed to make the necessary repairs or improvements, and schedule times to buy or rent the supplies or equipment.

- Designate one weekend per month as home improvement weekend. (Obviously, you can do it more or less often depending on your needs.)

- If you never feel like making home repairs or renovations on the weekend, try doing them at a different time. It's kind of silly that millions of people ruin their weekends worrying about the projects they should be doing but aren't doing. Nothing says that a loose doorknob or leaky pipe can't be fixed on a Wednesday.

- Keep the phone numbers and business cards of repair people in one visible spot so that you'll be less likely to put off calling someone to do the work.

- If you put off having repairs or renovations done because it's hard to schedule time away from work or other commitments so you can be at home, contact the National Association of Professional Organizers (www.napo.net) to find any members in your area who offer concierge services. What that means is that the professional organizer or someone on his or her staff can come sit at your house to wait for a repairperson, oversee the work, and handle any other details involved.

Yard Work

Let me begin this section by making an important distinction: Yard work is not gardening. Yard work is all that mundane, repetitive maintenance you have to do, such as cutting the grass, trimming hedges, watering plants, raking leaves, and weeding. Yard work is what you do to keep your neighbors from mistaking your family for the Munsters. Gardening, on the other hand, is fun (at least it is to a lot of people). You get to plant pretty flowers, be creative with landscaping designs, and nurture little seedlings into sturdy trees and bushes. Many people find the time to plant petunias, but then can't seem to find the time or desire to water them.

ACTION TACTIC

To get motivated to do yard work and to get ideas for the fun parts (gardening), check out all the neat information, tips, and timesavers at www.gardenweb.com.

The reasons for procrastinating about yard work are much the same as for other household chores. It doesn't seem as urgent as some indoor tasks; it's often messy and strenuous; you may not have the right supplies or equipment, or the ones you have are hard to get to in a crowded garage or tool shed. Plus, it usually seems to be hot and sticky or cold and rainy when yard work begs to be done.

Solutions for getting it done are also similar to those for other chores: delegate it whenever possible, schedule it into your routine so that it becomes a habit, and keep your supplies in good working order and easily accessible. To minimize the problem in the first place, keep your lawn as low-maintenance as possible so that there's less to do or to put off doing.

The Least You Need to Know

- You may never grow to love housework, but you can make it easier with a few simple techniques.
- Getting rid of clutter, organizing supplies, and using the chip-away technique makes it easier to do any chore.
- Getting laundry and dry cleaning done and taking out the trash is a matter of finding more convenient ways to do them.
- Chores like home repairs and yard work are easier to get done when you delegate them or schedule times to do them.

Procrastination in Your Family and Social Life

In This Chapter

- Saying I do or I don't
- Making the baby decision
- Putting the social back in your social life

Noted anthropologist Margaret Mead was once quoted as saying, "No matter how many communes anybody invents, the family always creeps back." There does seem to be some truth in that statement. Maybe having people connected to us by blood or bound by a legal document is a deep-seated survival strategy. Perhaps it's a biological need to procreate. Whatever it is, something draws many people to marriage and children, or just to connecting with each other socially. Despite the draw, however, good old procrastination often gets in the way.

Marriage, American Style

Year after year, U.S. Census Bureau statistics reveal that married adults are the majority in this country. If marriage is that common, why do we hear about so many people dragging their feet on the road to matrimony?

Some instances of marriage-related procrastination can be attributed to societal conditions that fuel it, such as more widespread acceptance of living together without marriage or getting married at a later age than in past decades. But the rest of it is undoubtedly due to what's going on in the minds of these bachelors and bachelorettes. As with any other sort of procrastination, fears, anxiety, and misconceptions can cause people to delay making the commitment to a lifetime together. If you're experiencing cold feet when it comes to marriage, or you feel a chilly draft on the way, see whether any of these common causes apply to you:

- Having concerns about long-range compatibility with your partner

- Not being ready to give up the freedom of single life

- Looking for perfection in your partner or in the relationship

- Not knowing what you want out of life

- Having lousy decision-making skills

- Making the commitment aspect of marriage more overwhelming than it needs to be

- Being frightened by the statistic that half of all marriages end in divorce

- Being too comfortable with the status quo in your relationship to feel the impetus to take the next step

- Not feeling settled or secure enough in your career or finances to merge your life with someone else's

QUICKSAND!

If it's your partner, not you, who is procrastinating making the marriage (or the living-as-married) commitment, be careful how you use your powers of persuasion. Nagging, badgering, and being demanding or manipulative won't get you anywhere.

Because marriage is one of the biggest commitments you'll ever make, it's a good thing to have these concerns. You obviously need to give a great deal of thought to the decision. On the other hand, if your tendency is to procrastinate when it comes to any difficult decisions in life, then you need to distinguish between being careful and being indecisive.

Saying "I Do," Not "I'll Do It Later"

You can make the marriage decision easier by asking yourself three questions and offering yourself the following solutions:

1. Do I have doubts about my long-range compatibility with my partner?

    If the problem lies with the nature of the relationship itself and with the doubt that you can love, honor, and cherish this particular person from here to eternity, then you need to address that problem head-on. Talk to your partner about your doubts. If the attachment is meant to be, it can withstand what might be a very difficult discussion. If the problems are too big for the two of you to sort out on your own, consider talking them through with a counselor who specializes in relationships before you write off the relationship as doomed.

2. Do I know what I want out of life and out of a life partner?

    Before you can make a life with someone, you have to know what kind of life you want. You need to have a handle on what's important to you, how you want to spend your time each day, and what your long-range goals are before you can venture into marriage with confidence.

3. Is this yet another example of my difficulty with making decisions?

    You might be in a wonderful, solid relationship, adore your partner, and value the institution of marriage, but your lack of decision-making skill is keeping you from taking the next step. If that's the case, then try to zero in on how and why you might be making the decision harder than it needs to be, and use the techniques suggested in Chapter 7.

Putting Off the Pitter-Patter

It is easy to get so caught up in living your life and doing your job that you can realize quite suddenly that the window of opportunity for starting a family is closing. Whether it's a woman's biological clock or either partner's desire to raise kids while still young enough to chase after them, time and age are factors when making the baby decision.

YOU'RE NOT ALONE

Who of us is mature enough for offspring before the offspring themselves arrive? The value of marriage is not that adults produce children but that children produce adults.

—Peter de Vries, twentieth-century American novelist

Because time is of the essence, you'd think people wouldn't put off making the decision, but, of course, procrastinators always find a way. This is usually where the classic excuse, "It's not the right time" pops up. Here are some typical reasons why healthy women and men might feel it's not the right time to have a baby:

- Being too busy in a career or not yet having reached certain professional goals

- Not being financially secure enough

- Not having adequate health insurance

- Not having a home that's spacious enough or set up right for kids, or not feeling settled in one geographic location

- Not being ready to give up the freedom of a childless life

- Not being ready or willing to give up habits like smoking and drinking (in the case of the prospective mother, although this can apply to the father as well)

- Not being in good enough physical shape (again, this applies mostly to the mother, but it can be an issue for the daddy-to-be also)

- Doubting your parenting capabilities or even doubting how much you like kids in the first place

ACTION TACTIC

If you're concerned about being financially ready for a family, go to www.babycenter.com, which has a nifty tool to help you calculate the cost of baby's first year.

What's interesting about this list is that these reasons are all much more valid than the usual excuses for procrastinating. After all, deciding to have a child is just as great a commitment as deciding to marry, probably more so. Having doubts is a good thing. If you look at all the cons, not just the pros, before you decide, you'll have a better idea of what you're getting into and whether bringing a child into your world is the right thing to do.

So how do you decide? First, recognize that only you and your partner (or you alone, if you plan to be a single parent) can make that decision. To make it a little easier, and to help yourself make the right decision, don't just look inward, but look for input from outside as well. Reading books on parenting, spending time with other people's kids (the brats and the angels), getting some hard data on the cost of raising a child, having a pre-pregnancy checkup with a physician or certified nurse midwife, meeting with a nutritionist—all these efforts can help you take an objective look at what's involved and whether it's the right move for you. Beyond that, you have to listen to what your heart is telling you to do.

Get a Life—Socially Speaking

So you want to make a change in your social life. Maybe you've recently ended a relationship or marriage and want to meet someone new or haven't been in a relationship at all in quite a while. Perhaps your spouse or partner passed away some time ago, and you now feel ready to date again. Whatever the situation, you might say that you'd like to date more and meet someone special, but the procrastinator in you comes up with all sorts of excuses for why you don't have the time, why it's not the right time, or why you shouldn't do it.

YOU'RE NOT ALONE

If my wife and I don't book a baby sitter in advance, we end up not going out. It's not that the sitters' schedules are the problem. It's that we use baby sitting as an excuse to be lazy. If we wait to the last minute, we say, "Oh we probably can't get a sitter, so let's stay in." But if one is on the calendar, we go.

—Mohammad M., banker

Or maybe socializing for you is less about meeting Mr. or Ms. Right and more about just having fun and a change of pace. You might even be married or seriously involved with someone already but have a social life that consists of nothing more than cozying up to a rented video and take-out food every Friday night. There's nothing wrong with relaxing that way, whether you're single or attached, but when those quiet evenings at home start to feel like a rut, it's time to make some changes. You might say that you'd like to get out more, do new things, and meet new people, but your procrastination habit causes you to let work or family demands keep you stuck in that unsocial rut.

You know you're in trouble when you're starting to remember the puzzles on *Wheel of Fortune* reruns or when your closest friend is the guy who delivers take-out food to your office while you burn the midnight oil night after night. Whether your problem is having no life or having only a work life, it's easy to find yourself doing the same old thing day after day. You end up falling out of touch with old friends and not making new ones, and have more dates with the television and a bag of chips than with live human beings.

If you're not getting out to have a social life, the issue may be time or even lack of organization. You don't seem to have enough of it to get all your responsibilities out of the way and still have some time left over for fun. This is particularly true for people with demanding careers and/or busy family lives. Be sure to follow the tips in Chapter 5.

ACTION TACTIC

To motivate yourself to get out of a rut and into having more fun, read *Beyond Love and Work: Why Adults Need to Play* by Lenore Terr, MD. This fascinating book takes a scholarly yet practical look at how important it is to lose ourselves and find freedom in the act of play, just as we did when we were kids.

The problem might also stem from fears or feelings of insecurity about how effective you can be at meeting new people or developing relationships or friendships. No matter what the cause, try to spur yourself into action with the following strategies:

- **Make it a priority.** If you don't make a conscious effort on a daily basis to be on the lookout for opportunities to socialize and to make the necessary plans, then week after week will pass by with no change in your social life.

- **Make advance plans.** If you schedule get-togethers with friends, reply early to party invitations, and make advance reservations for meals or events, you'll be more likely to stick with those plans. Without a clear plan, you can give in to excuses like, "I just don't feel up to going out tonight," or "I'll see them next week." Even better, buy nonrefundable tickets to events far in advance so that you'll have more incentive to honor your commitment to go.

- **Combine socializing with another activity.** If finding spare time is a major problem, look for activities that have double rewards. If you'd like to get more exercise, consider group sports or group outings such as organized hikes or bike rides, where you can get in shape and meet people at the same time. If there's something you'd like to learn or a skill you want to brush up on, take a course; it's a chance to make some new friends and socialize after class.

- **Work on your social skills.** Some social butterflies do seem to have a natural gift of gab and an innate ability to maneuver any social situation, but that doesn't mean social relations skills can't be learned by the more introverted among us. Adult learning centers and some universities' night schools offer courses in such fine academic pursuits as the art of flirting, how to talk to anybody anywhere, and how to attract the opposite sex.

- **Make a point of following through.** How many times have you met a nice person, exchanged phone numbers, said you'd call or email each other next week to get together, and then never laid eyes on each other again? A quick fix is to exchange contact information on the spot—put the other person's number in your phone, send each other a text right away so the dialogue is already started even while still face to face, or send out an immediate LinkedIn or Facebook connection invitation while still with each other.

- **Socialize online.** As long as you tread carefully with your personal safety at the forefront of everything you do, your social life can be vastly improved by moving it online. Whether you simply expand your social networks or join dating sites, socializing online is a convenient, less intimidating way to get to know someone or to stay in touch with someone you already know before investing time offline.

ACTION TACTIC

When you meet someone new, try to get an email address in addition to, or instead of, a phone number. Then, if you're hesitant to pick up the phone and call the person for fear that the person might not want to hear from you, or if you feel a text might be too intrusive, you can use the less direct (and therefore less intimidating) method of emailing first.

Saying I Don't

Just about everyone (except maybe those who marry their high school sweetheart and live happily ever after) has had the experience of staying in a relationship or marriage far too long. You may know the feeling; something's just not quite right, and the relationship doesn't seem to have any future, but you put off doing anything about it. Or, if married, you might be very unhappy, but upsetting the status quo seems simply too huge of a project, emotionally and logistically. It often seems easier to stick it out than to make the tough decisions and have the difficult discussions necessary to make the relationship or marriage better or leave it confidently.

This dilemma is expressed well in the book *Too Good to Leave, Too Bad to Stay: A Step-by-Step Guide to Help You Decide Whether to Stay In or Get Out of Your Relationship,* by Mira Kirshenbaum. Procrastinating taking a firm stand on where a relationship stands is the result of what she calls "relationship ambivalence."

YOU'RE NOT ALONE

I keep trying to convince myself that with time my so-called soul mate will change. He says things like, "Hang in there—don't give up on me." But who's hanging in there with me? I'm just a maternal push-over, always there for someone else and too tired to soul search, so I keep putting off doing anything about the relationship.

—Harriette S., administrative assistant

When in this ambivalent state, you do all the wrong things to try to make decisions about whether to cut loose or stay and try to make the relationship work. This list is a synopsis of those wrong things, described in more detail in Kirshenbaum's book:

- You go through long stretches of bad times and ill will in the relationship, but then the atmosphere changes, the outlook is rosy again, and you sweep the problems under the rug until the next time they pop up.

- You complain about the relationship or the other person but contradict yourself by saying you don't want to leave.

- You talk to everyone about the problem, hoping someone will tell you what to do.

- You obsess over the problem, thinking and worrying about it constantly, but you don't take any action.

- You assume that the matter is just about your own fear of commitment, or fear of being on your own if already married, not a problem with the relationship itself.

- You wait for some sort of sign, the lightbulb over the head to go on, that will tell you what to do.

- You take an overly rational, objective approach, listing the pros and cons, assigning each a rating, and hoping that with enough number-crunching you'll come up with the answer.

- You keep leaving, hoping that breaking up or separating will stir things up or improve the situation, but it doesn't, and you always come back to give the other person yet another second chance.

Instead of relying on those ineffective or hit-or-miss approaches, try instead to diagnose the problem step by step as a physician would diagnose a physical ailment. Try to remove yourself from the situation (mentally, that is) enough to cast an objective eye on it and to take all factors into account while still letting your gut feelings have a say in the matter.

Most likely, though, you will need to seek help from a mental health counselor who specializes in relationships or marriage. These sorts of decisions are often difficult to make on your own or with your partner alone, and if children are involved in a marriage, the decision to say "I don't" instead of sticking with the "I do" vows is critical. So to stop procrastinating, connect with the information and people who can help you through the process.

The Least You Need to Know

- Putting off marriage results from practical concerns, such as money matters, as well as fears and doubts.
- Putting off the decision to start a family is an example of good procrastination, because such a major commitment requires careful thought.
- Getting stuck in a social life rut is often caused by not making it a priority and by anxieties about putting yourself out there.
- Deciding whether to stay in or end a relationship or marriage is made easier when you seek professional counseling and is too important not to.

Procrastination in Everyday Life Matters

In This Chapter

- How to keep a New Year's resolution beyond January 2
- Tending to your health
- Facing up to grown-up stuff like death, taxes, and money

Isn't it amazing how easy it is to put off the things in life that are the most important for your security and well-being? We all know that without good health, life isn't all that it could or should be. And everybody knows how important it is to pay bills on time, plan for a financially secure future, file income taxes, and have an up-to-date will. But does everyone do all these things—or do them in a timely manner? Hardly.

The fact that so many people procrastinate about critical matters is proof that fear of negative consequences is not always enough of a motivator to spark action. This chapter helps you find other ways to do something about the problem.

Why New Year's Resolutions Lose Their Resolve

Quick: name one New Year's resolution you've ever kept all year or even longer. Still thinking? Nothing coming to mind? That's what I figured.

Not keeping New Year's resolutions is not just a matter of self-discipline and willpower. It is in large part a procrastination problem. You say you're going to turn over a new leaf on January 1, but when that day arrives, you don't quite feel ready. You decide it would be better to wait and turn over that new leaf after the Super Bowl, or when the winter doldrums pass and spring kicks in, or when all the holiday leftovers have been eaten, or when work slows down, or when, well, you get the picture. Before you know it, it's pretty clear that you're not going to quit smoking, stop biting your nails, lose weight, learn to speak Urdu, or whatever it is you want to do, until hell freezes over.

YOU'RE NOT ALONE

I think I procrastinate in my personal life because I'm so overwhelmingly busy with a full-time career and a part-time business that when it comes to doing things for myself, I put them off. In my work, I can't miss deadlines, so when I have a moment free, I hate to burden myself with something else to do.

—Fran K., communications manager

It's a miracle that any New Year's resolutions are ever kept. When you make one, you expect dramatic changes to take place in your behavior overnight. Think about how silly it is that you could be one person on December 31 (and all the days that came before) and a totally different person on January 1. As you found out in Chapter 4, change happens gradually and requires a shift in both mindset and daily routine.

There are five main flaws in most people's New Year's resolutions:

- The resolution is not linked to specific behavioral changes and actions to take—it's too broad.

- Your routine has not been adjusted to make the behavioral change a priority use of your time so it slips through the cracks, or you make excuses about not having time for it.

- You give in to all-or-nothing thinking, forgetting that a resolution is a behavioral change, and that changes happen gradually and setbacks are normal.

- You have failed with resolutions so many prior years that you've internalized the belief that you will never keep one.

- You let your mind play so many tricks on you that you get outsmarted by your "primitive" brain telling you in the moment to go for the fun stuff, the easy stuff, the good stuff, instead of sticking it out by doing (or resisting) the more difficult tasks for delayed, future rewards.

In the next section, we look at ways to counter these problems so that you don't go yet another year without reaching your goals.

How to Keep Your New Year's Resolutions

All the usual strategies for overcoming procrastination work for most New Year's resolutions. But the ones that are particularly appropriate for resolutions are described here.

When the resolution is too broad ... If you say, "I want to lose weight this year," or even if you're more specific with a resolution like, "I want to lose 20 pounds by summer," the statement is too general. Those are goals or end results. They're not resolutions. A resolution is the act of resolving to do something specific. You resolve to eat fast food only once a week instead four or five times a week. You resolve to join a weight-loss group on Monday morning. Resolutions will work only if you make them concrete, specific, and doable. Start with a simple baby step you can achieve on January 1. Then with the confidence and momentum built from that accomplishment, set the next step for a week later, or whatever time frame makes sense. Keep going with weekly or monthly resolutions until you reach the ultimate goal.

When the resolution doesn't get worked into daily life ... You might have so much determination to keep your resolution that it's practically spilling out of you. But no matter how much you are psychologically ready to work toward your goals, you won't reach them unless your daily routine incorporates the steps necessary for reaching those goals. As you learned in Chapter 5, extra time doesn't appear out of nowhere. If you resolve, for example, to spend less time working and more time with your kids, that resolution won't happen unless you take some pretty drastic measures to reorganize your work and home lives and rethink how you schedule your days. So think about what this resolution is going to entail, take a realistic look at your overall life commitments and your calendar, and figure out how you are going to fit in the actions that are necessary to keep this resolution.

When our resolutions are based on an all-or-nothing attitude ... When we're trying to make changes in our behavior, even the strongest of us develop very fragile egos. We set out toward our goals with the highest of hopes yet with nagging doubts about our ability to reach them. Then when we hit the first snag, our self-confidence is shattered. Instead of rolling with the punches and realizing that all change comes with setbacks and relapses, we let the setback get to us. We say, "It's hopeless. I'll never keep a New Year's resolution, so I'm not even going to try anymore."

When you've internalized a sense of failure ... After so many years of not keeping your New Year's resolutions, you may have internalized the past failures to the point that you have no confidence in your ability to stick with a resolution made for January 1. So why not break the cycle of failure and start making springtime resolutions, or July 4 resolutions, or whatever works for you and the situation? Stop looking at January 1 as the only magic date on the calendar!

When your mind is playing tricks on you ... Play tricks on it! In my own personal struggle to keep New Year's resolutions over the years, I've learned something that works. Yes, actually works. I trick myself into doing them. In one recent year I knew that I needed to lose some weight. I'd been great about keeping weight off for quite a number of years after letting middle-age pounds slip up on me, but one recent fall I picked up far more weight than I was comfortable with due to some extraordinary personal and work stress in my life. So as New Year's approached, I was tempted to make that tired old resolution, "I will lose weight." But instead, I played a trick on myself. I made this resolution: "Eat more kale."

I know, it sounds wacky. But here's why it worked. (Yes, it did work.) When I eat kale, I feel virtuous. I feel like I am in a healthy eating mode—because I am. Eating kale leads to eating spinach and bok choy and quinoa and broccoli and brown rice, and, well, the list goes on and on. And I keep the giant vegetable steamer out on the stove all the time instead of crammed into the pantry, so I can steam any leafy green vegetable any time without it being a big darn deal. And because steamed kale tastes just okay—not great—I also feel like if I've made myself eat it, I'm not going to blow my regime later on french fries. So think about one little step you can take to trick yourself into being on the path to keeping a resolution. Meanwhile, I'll just keep eating kale at least once a week and listening out for your own success stories.

QUICKSAND!

Waiting for the brink of a new year to make changes in your life or your behavior is a form of rationalized procrastination. Instead of making positive changes in the summer, fall, or any other time, you say, "I'll wait until January and make it a New Year's resolution." That's still procrastination any way you cut it. Don't fall for it. Start the change process whenever you need to and feel motivated to, even long before the next January 1.

Making Health-Care Appointments

You know that doctors, dentists, and other health professionals can make the hurt go away or can keep it from coming in the first place through preventive care. You know you're supposed to have regular checkups. You know you should be screened or immunized at certain ages for various conditions (for example, having mammograms, colonoscopies, cholesterol checks, and other pokes and prods most women and men would gladly put off). You know how important medical and dental care is, but you don't always get around to getting it, do you?

ACTION TACTIC

Find out if any of your medical providers are using NextMD (www. nextmd.com). This is a great site for booking appointments online and communicating with your doctor's office in a convenient, safe, and secure way 24/7. If your doctor uses NextMD and provides you with login information to enroll, you will have no excuses for procrastinating about your health care.

Here are some of the classic excuses, along with a reality check for each one:

"I feel fine. The doctor will only find something wrong."

Reality: If you're fine, that's what the doctor will find. If you're not fine, you should know about it before the problem goes undetected and worsens.

"There's no history of serious disease or illness in my family, so I don't have to worry."

Reality: Genetics play only a part in most major health problems. You can get breast cancer, colon cancer, and many other terrible diseases with no family history.

"The pain will go away."

Reality: And just how do you think that's going to happen? Maybe you can cover it up for a while, and maybe it will even disappear for a while, but like a bad debt and bad ex-lovers, pain usually comes back to haunt you.

"It won't make a difference. If I'm going to get cancer, I'm going to get it."

Reality: Of course it will make a difference. Early detection does wonders in improving your chances of surviving most treatable diseases. If you'd rather not undergo debilitating treatments for a terminal condition, no one can force you to.

"It hurts."

Reality: The things that doctors, dentists, physical therapists, and other health-care providers have to do to you sometimes don't exactly feel like lying in a bed of rose petals. But 9 times out of 10, the pain that comes with preventive care or treatment for a problem is much milder than what you'd experience if problems went undetected and untreated.

"I don't have time."

Reality: You do have the time for something this important.

"I don't like my doctor."

Reality: Get a new one. Even with health-care plans with limited choices, you usually do have at least a few doctors to select from.

"I don't know who to go to."

Reality: I know this is often a valid reason for delay. I know that frustrating feeling of randomly choosing a doctor out of a directory based on nothing more than the office location or how you like the sound of his or her name. You can make the process less haphazard by asking for referrals from friends and neighbors, and then seeing which ones are part of your health plan.

"My health plan/insurance doesn't cover it."

Reality: Most plans cover basic checkups and many tests. If you don't have health insurance or do but need to keep out-of-pocket expenses down, contact hospitals in your area, as well as your state's Department of Health, for suggestions of any free or low-cost services you might use.

You might find that none of the preceding excuses rings true for you. Maybe you don't have mental hang-ups or financial obstacles to seeking health care. Maybe you just don't get around to booking the appointments. To solve that problem, you can try a few strategies. First, when you leave one appointment, go ahead and book the next one, even if it's for a whole year away. You might end up needing to reschedule it closer to the time as you can't predict your own schedule that far in advance, but at least you have an appointment on the books as a starting point. Also, work these bookings into your calendar. Each December (or anytime if December is far away), schedule an appointment with yourself (an actual block of time on your calendar) when you will sit down and review your insurance coverage and think through all the appointments you need to schedule for the year, assuming you typically only need routine check-ups or other predictable appointments. Make sure you're doing this on a weekday during business hours so that you can immediately contact offices to get dates on your calendar.

YOU'RE NOT ALONE

It's unfortunate how many people put off exercising because of misperceptions about what's necessary to reach reasonable fitness goals. They assume they'll have to work out for hours on end, seven days a week, to get in shape, when, in fact, if they perform the movements they enjoy and exercise efficiently, two hours a week would probably do the trick.

—Tim Haft, president, Punk Rope (www.punkrope.com), New York City

Money Matters We Put Off and Why It Matters

Even though we know that—supposedly—love makes the world go 'round, ask any regular Joe or Josephine on the street what makes the world tick, and they'll probably tell you it's money. We know money doesn't buy happiness, but it can sure make life a little easier. So why do we make our lives harder by procrastinating when it comes to financial matters?

We complicate our lives by paying bills late, not getting around to budgeting or digging ourselves out of debt, delaying saving and investing, and keeping our financial records in disarray.

The price we pay for finance-related procrastination is, well, financial in that we pay penalties, late fees, and interest charges. We shortchange ourselves by ending up with not enough money to retire comfortably on or, even long before retirement, just not tracking what goes out and what goes in well enough to be able to spend some fun money here and there. And we pay the price psychologically with excessive worry, anxiety, and uncertainty.

ACTION TACTIC

If lack of knowledge is holding you back from getting your finances under control (your control!), turn to consumer expert Clark Howard to learn how to save more, spend less, and avoid getting ripped off (www. clarkhoward.com).

Why We Procrastinate About Money Matters

As with procrastination in all areas of life, the causes, and therefore the solutions, can be found by looking internally and externally. External factors play a particularly big role in the putting off of money matters. Our finances inevitably come with lots of paperwork. Increasingly, that paper is electronic rather than the physical kind that clutters our file cabinets and creates piles on our desks. But any way you cut it, there are documents, statements, prospectuses, receipts, and much more that we have to keep track of, whether online or off. That lack of organization makes for one tall obstacle when it's time to file tax returns, prepare a budget, pay bills, or do major financial planning. Instead of chasing down all the documentation and figures you need, it's easier to say, "I'll deal with it later."

YOU'RE NOT ALONE

It isn't enough for you to love money—it's also necessary that money should love you.

—Baron Rothschild, eighteenth-century British nobleman and member of the Rothschild banking family

Then there are the internal factors. Twentieth-century poet Carl Sandburg was quoted as saying, "Money is power, freedom, a cushion, the root of all evil, the sum of blessings." I think what he was saying is that money can make us crazy. As with any type of procrastination, putting off dealing with your finances often has less to do with a lack of organization or knowledge and more to do with your emotional battle with money.

QUICKSAND!

This chapter does not take the place of expert advice on such issues as financial planning, tax preparation, or writing wills. Entire books focus on those complex topics. The emphasis in this chapter is on identifying your mental and environmental blocks to taking care of these matters and on strategies for getting past those blocks. Then when you're ready to take action, you can turn to the many resources available online and to qualified financial and legal advisors.

What to Do About Your Financial Procrastination

Just as the causes of procrastination about money matters mirror those of any type of procrastination, the solutions can be found in many of the strategies already described (especially those in Chapter 8). In addition, consider these techniques for getting yourself out of the red and financially ahead:

- Overcome a lack of organization. For financial documents you must keep in paper form, use the stacking tray, sorting, and filing techniques described in Chapter 6. Also, scan as much as you can and keep it in a secure location in your computer. And try to avoid paper as much as possible by going digital with your finances, including electronic bank or investment statements and alerts of bills due, paying bills online, and keeping your budget in personal finance software such as Quicken (http://quicken.intuit.com) or a financial website such as Mint (www.mint.com).

- Get past a lack of knowledge. If no one has ever taught you how to keep your finances in order, plan a budget, handle credit responsibly, and invest wisely, you can't be expected to know how to do those things. There's nothing wrong with not knowing how to do something. There is something wrong with putting off making an effort to learn what you need to know, or, when possible, to hire someone to do what you don't know how to do. That's what financial planners, debt counselors, and others who make it their business to keep up to speed on money matters are there for.

YOU'RE NOT ALONE

Carrying around all the debts I have is like walking around with a 100-pound weight hanging from my neck. I worry about them every day, but I don't do anything about it. I say it's because I don't have the money to pay them off, but I know there must be ways around that. But now the problem has built up so much I feel like I'll never dig myself out of the hole.

—Lee M., editor

- Outsmart the mind games. Until you can identify and deal with the irrational, self-defeating thoughts at the root of your money problems, the best nuts-and-bolts financial strategies in the world won't help you. Start with telling yourself that sticking your head in the sand and not worrying about retirement or the debts that are piling up is not a strategy. You might feel better temporarily—denial is really good for that—but sooner or later you'll pay the price, in both peace of mind and money or quality of life.

Next, banish the all-or-nothing thinking. Your debts might be so overwhelming that you don't know where to begin so you don't even try. But use the chip-away technique—paying a little here and a little there when you can to start making a dent. And don't use all-or-nothing thinking when contemplating the future. You're not too young or too old to save and invest. Any time is the right time.

QUICKSAND!

If you prepare a budget but never look at it again, it's of no use to you. Don't go to all the trouble to make a budget only to bury it in a forgotten folder on your hard drive or in the dark recesses of a file cabinet drawer. Keep it close at hand so that you'll have a constant reminder of what you should be doing with your money.

Making Taxes Less Taxing

Each year as April 15 approaches, the U.S. Postal Service expects tens of millions of last-minute income tax filers. Many locations around the country extend post office hours to accommodate these procrastinators. Even local businesses get in on the act. Festivities in past years have included the following:

- A Harrisburg, Pennsylvania, post office welcomed taxpayers with the world's "Largest IRS Tax Loophole," composed of 1,040 red, white, and blue balloons in the shape of an arch.

- The worst procrastinator in Charleston, West Virginia, received a trophy from the Charleston Postmaster.

- A local radio station broadcasting live from the San Francisco Processing and Distribution Center paid the taxes of one lucky listener.

- The Leslie Gore tune, "It's My Party (and I'll Cry If I Want To)," rang out in the lobby of a Springfield, Illinois, post office on tax night, courtesy of a local oldies radio station. A disc jockey handed out tax relief packages of Rolaids and aspirin to Springfield customers "Crying" along with Roy Orbison over their 1040s.

MATTER OF FACT

Taxes may be the last thing on your mind during the lazy, hazy days of summer, but summer is one of the best times to think about them. Doing so gives you a chance to make financial adjustments while there's still time. You can review any new tax-break legislation, and if you're paying estimated taxes, you can look at your year-to-date income to see whether you're paying enough. You'll also still have several months to plan any charitable donations and to make contributions to retirement plans or other investment accounts.

Clearly, the last-minute tax rush can look like more of a party than a bunch of frazzled citizens fulfilling their civic duty. But what if it's a party you'd rather not attend? If you'd like to get over your taxing procrastination, try these tactics:

- Break down the project of preparing and filing into steps (such as obtain forms, assemble records, prepare information, and set an appointment with a tax preparer). Make a list of the steps involved.

- File electronically! More than 100 million taxpayers already do, and at some point in the future—perhaps by the time you're reading this—e-filing might be made mandatory by the IRS. Filing electronically saves many steps typically involved in the paper method. And even though everybody still has the same April 15 deadline whether filing by mail or online, the timesaving aspects of e-filing do give you a little extra time.

- Focus on do dates, not the due date. Forget about April 15 for a while and instead schedule dates and times to take care of each step in the process leading up to April 15.

- Keep your financial records well organized so that you won't have to dread rounding up all the information you need. Using personal finance software or an online service can come in particularly handy at tax time as you can often have much of your data automatically fed into an online tax service such as TurboTax (www.turbotax.com) or provided to your accountant.

- Don't wait for the motivation or desire to do your taxes, because it may never come. Just accept that you have to do them whether you want to or not.

- If possible, have a qualified tax preparer do them for you, and don't wait until the last minute to contact that person or you might end up having to pay higher fees for a rush job.

- Get past any emotional resentment toward the IRS. Nobody likes to pay taxes, and many of us resent some of the things that our tax dollars are used for. But if you think that holding off until 11:59 P.M. on April 15 is sending a message to the government, forget about it. You're only inconveniencing and stressing yourself out.

- Make a fun plan with friends or family, preferably the sort of thing you have to buy tickets for in advance, for the evenings of April 14 and 15, so you'll have an incentive to be finished by then.

The filing of income taxes rolls around every year whether you like it or not. So there's really no excuse to procrastinate. Take some time long before April 15 to get organized, put some good systems in place, consult with any experts you need help from, and put some do dates on your calendar. Once you've done that for one year, you'll thank yourself in all the subsequent years when tax time rolls around and you can relax.

Dealing with the Reality of Mortality

As the saying goes, only two things in life are guaranteed: death and taxes. We know why you put off dealing with taxes; now let's look at why you procrastinate dealing with death—or at least the paperwork you need on the subject of death. Have you been delaying putting together or updating a will or doing some serious estate planning? If so, you're not alone. According to a recent Harris poll for Martindale-Hubbell, more than half of all adults in the United States do not have a will. Have you been procrastinating for any of these reasons?

- You don't think you have enough assets to warrant estate planning.

- You're too young to worry about it. It's not an urgent priority.

- You don't like to make the sorts of big decisions that writing your will or estate planning would require you to make.

- You figure it will all go to the government anyway, so why bother?

- You don't want to hurt anyone's feelings by excluding them from your will or giving them less than others.

- You don't like to think about dying.

- You're superstitious; if you write a will, you'll die soon after.

- You can't afford to work with an attorney.

YOU'RE NOT ALONE

We'd been meaning to write wills since our first daughter was born six years ago, but weren't sure who to name as guardians. Plus, we couldn't quite face the thought of dying. Two things finally kick-started us. My brother got married, providing us with perfect guardians. And we felt the need to scratch out last-minute wills before a helicopter ride in Hawaii!

—Becky A., technical writer

Valid excuses? Not really. If you die intestate, which means without a will, the state determines what happens with your money and property. In most cases, the laws dictate that your estate goes to your spouse and children, if you have them. That may sound fine, but how do you know they'll divide it up the way you would want? And what if you're single? How does the state know you would want some of your assets to go to your favorite charity or that your book collection should go to your best friend and your big-screen television to your couch-potato cousin?

QUICKSAND!

If you really don't want to be a procrastinator, you can make arrangements and prepayments for your funeral long before you die so that your loved ones won't have to deal with all that. Beware of con artists, though. Scams are all too common. If in doubt, check out the National Funeral Directors Association's *Consumer Tips on Prepaying Your Funeral* at www.nfda.org or call 800-228-6332 for assistance.

Some people only need to write a simple will. But others, with more significant assets, need to do estate planning with the help of attorneys and financial advisors. Estate planning helps you control what happens to your assets after you die so that you—not the IRS or the courts—choose what happens to all you have worked so hard to build. There are also potential tax benefits for your heirs. Proper estate planning can reduce or even eliminate estate taxation, and in some cases actually builds wealth for your heirs. Don't you owe it to your heirs or to charitable organizations you care about to take care of this now?!

YOU'RE NOT ALONE

Ten years ago when I remarried, it crossed my mind that if something happened to me, would my husband know what sentimental items I'd want passed on to my three daughters? We talked about wills then, again three years later when I got pregnant, bought software to make wills two years later, reminded ourselves each year after that, but haven't done it. I think it's procrastination of facing the inevitable—death.

—Cynthia D., professional counselor

The Least You Need to Know

- New Year's resolutions often aren't kept because we expect dramatic changes too quickly and we don't define precisely enough what it is we're going to do to bring about change.
- Investing a little time and money in preventive health care can save you a lot of time and money—and pain—in the long run.
- Putting off dealing with finances and taxes usually results from lack of organization, lack of knowledge, or emotional issues with money.
- You may not want to think about death, but estate planning and will preparation can let you rest in peace when the time comes.

Procrastination at Work and School

In This Chapter

- Getting out of a career rut
- How to stop putting off a job search
- Proactive career-management strategies
- Stop procrastinating in high school, college, and grad school

If I were to take a peek at your work or school to-do list, what would I find? A report due tomorrow that you haven't started? Papers to grade? A professional certification overdue for renewal? A difficult conversation you need to have with an employee that you keep putting off? An exam you haven't cracked a book for? Graduate school applications you haven't had time to complete?

You'd think that with the stakes as high as they are in our jobs and education, we'd stay on top of everything. Well, we don't. Studies have repeatedly shown that 80 to 95 percent of students procrastinate, with up to a quarter of those doing it regularly. And when it comes to workplace procrastination, experts agree that millions of people do it, on occasion or chronically. This chapter teaches you what to do about it so you won't be putting that paycheck or diploma in jeopardy.

A Career in Procrastination

For many people, jobs are more than a way to earn a living. They're the building blocks of a career, the collection of work experiences over a life span that make up a part of one's identity and can be a major source of satisfaction and fulfillment in life. Career-related procrastination can have the following results:

- Getting stuck in a job or career field you don't enjoy or value

- Not reaching your full potential

- Earning less money than you could if you were to make some changes in your job or career

- Waiting so long to make a career change that the transition is more difficult and time-consuming than it would have been if you'd done it sooner

- Feeling insecure and uncertain about your job security and career future because you haven't set goals and worked toward them

- Not gaining the flexibility and independence that can come from self-employment (if that's something you desire)

YOU'RE NOT ALONE

Putting off focusing on my career has been my biggest procrastination problem. I've been going through life as if there were all the time in the world to make career decisions. In hindsight, I've realized that the act of not making a choice turns out to be a choice after all—and it's a choice I would not have made if I'd known the consequences.

—April R., artist/paralegal/office administrator

Many procrastinators are aware of those consequences, but they still can't seem to get moving in a new career direction.

Why Careers Stagnate

The reasons people put off making career decisions and acting upon them closely parallel those for any type of procrastination. You might find yourself overwhelmed by the many career options to choose from, underwhelmed by too few choices, or concerned by how much work is involved in making a career transition or trying to get a promotion. Or maybe you're reasonably comfortable in your same old job and career field and don't feel an urgent need to make career change a priority, even though, in the back of your mind, you think you'd be happier doing something else. Fear can also be a factor in that you might be nervous about venturing into the uncharted territory of a new career field or employer, interviewing again after a long absence from the job-hunting scene, or returning to school if that's a necessary step in your transition.

MATTER OF FACT

Some career indecision results from perfectionism, which in this case means feeling that you have to make the perfect choice that will keep you happy the rest of your life. The fact is, very few, if any, career decisions are irreversible, and statistics show that most people have several different careers over a lifetime. If you use effective transition strategies, it's never too late to make a career change, and you're never too deeply entrenched in one field or industry to switch to another.

Whether you're a student or recent grad choosing your first career, a parent looking to get back into the work world, or an experienced worker wanting to make a change, try the following strategies to motivate yourself:

* Realize that there is a method to the madness when choosing a career. You can learn this method by reading books about career planning or by working with a career development professional one on one or in seminars.

* Don't take the stab-in-the-dark approach. Many people who need to choose a new career go online and browse job postings. They start applying for jobs before they've even zeroed in on their overall career goals. Choose a direction first, and then look for jobs within that field or industry.

> **QUICKSAND!**
>
> Don't put off making decisions about a career direction just because you're waiting to find your calling. You might think that the perfect career choice will miraculously come to you some day, but that happens for very few people. You're more likely to choose a career based on a methodical process of elimination than by feeling a calling toward one occupation.

Don't forget that Chapter 4 discusses your options for a career coach or counselor to help you through this process.

Get a Job (and Love It)

It's the stuff of songs and movies. It's a source of friction between parents and their grown kids and among couples. It makes students want to stay in school forever and rattles the nerves of middle-agers with mortgages and orthodontists' bills. What is it? It's the prospect of getting a job and keeping it.

All but the independently wealthy, or successful entrepreneurs, rely on a job to put food on the table and a roof over their heads. Most people, of course, hope to do more than that. They hope to bring in enough income to be comfortable, or more than comfortable, not merely enough to eke out an existence. They'd even like to enjoy what they're doing while earning those dollars. This puts a lot of pressure on you not only to get a job, but also to get a good one and keep it. And anywhere there's pressure, there's likely to be procrastination.

You know you want a new job, a better job, or any old job, but you can't seem to do anything about it. One obvious reason for your procrastination may be that you don't enjoy job hunting. There's the prospect of long nights at the computer cranking out cover letters and fishing through job postings that don't interest you. There's the need to network with people and feel like you're always asking for favors. There are the cattle calls at employment agencies, the brush-offs from headhunters, and the rejections after interviews you thought you aced. To add insult to injury, you end up stuck with a big dry-cleaning tab. Job hunting doesn't have to be as miserable as all that; some people find it kind of interesting, even a little fun. But any way you cut it, pounding the pavement (more likely to be the cyberpavement these days with so much online job hunting and social networking) is not how most people would choose to spend their time.

Let's look at strategies for combating procrastination in your job search.

QUICKSAND!

Don't mistake this for a how-to-find-a-job chapter. The focus here is on the mental and situational obstacles that might cause you to put off looking for a job or to delay thinking about ensuring your job security. For the nuts and bolts of how to write résumés, interview, network, or devise a job search strategy, turn to recommended books, including *Find a Job Through Social Networking* by Crompton and Sautter, or my own *Unofficial Guide to Landing a Job!*

Too Comfortable to Leave, Too Miserable to Stay

When I was in private practice as a career counselor, I often received frantic calls from new or current clients saying that they couldn't stand their jobs anymore and needed to leave immediately and needed to see me immediately to discuss how to find a new one. Or they were certain that they were about to be caught up in a downsizing and needed to see me right away to line up a new job (if only it were that simple!). Invariably, when those same people would arrive in my office days later, all sense of urgency was gone. Maybe the day of the call had turned out to be only an isolated bad day. Or maybe they looked at their bank balance and realized that unemployment wouldn't help their bottom line, so they were no longer so eager to jump ship. Or perhaps they'd learned that impending layoffs were only a rumor and so their job was safe.

It's always nice to know that you've dodged a bullet this time, but when you give up that sense of urgency, you give in to the comfort factor: the fact that it's often easier to stay in a familiar situation than to venture into uncharted territory, even if the status quo is less than perfect.

Here's the solution: every time you hear yourself about to say, "I'll worry about a job later," remember how you felt the last time you were fed up with your job, or the last time you were laid off and unprepared to search for a new one. The idea is to relive that moment, however painful, until you get revved up again.

Fishing with a Net

Some people put off looking for a job, or give up too soon after starting, because they're going about it the wrong way. They start by putting out a few feelers. Maybe they answer a few job ads and don't get a reply, or they slap together a quick LinkedIn profile and nobody flocks to it. After a few days or weeks, or even a few months, of these flash-in-the-pan efforts, they assume that there's just not a better job out there and give up.

Here's the solution: Haphazard, passive approaches to getting a job rarely yield positive results. To motivate yourself from the start and to stay that way, you have to understand that a job search takes time and effort. You have to put thought into developing an effective strategy and make it a priority to implement that strategy every day.

QUICKSAND!

Don't get hung up trying to write the perfect résumé and never make it past that point to launching the job search. Your résumé is very important (as are your online profiles), but it's easy to drag out the process, writing draft after draft, getting way too many people's opinions on it, and taking too long to say, "It's done." Be honest with yourself and make sure you're not dwelling on the résumé just to avoid diving into the actual search.

No Target to Hit

Behind the haphazard fishing with a net approach to finding a new job is often a problem of not having a job target. Some people put off looking for a job because they don't know what to look for. This can be an example of the good kind of procrastination. If you don't know what you want in terms of an ideal type of employer, job duties, salary, and other characteristics, then you don't know where to begin looking because you don't have a clue about what you're looking for.

Take some time to zero in on a target and then your search will be much easier.

Job-Hunting Mind Games

As a job hunter you might be feeling a great deal of anxiety. You might have doubts about your ability to obtain, or succeed in, a new job. You may feel self-conscious about a scattered or lackluster employment history or nervous that a volatile former boss will give you a bad reference. You might feel ill at ease in interviews where it sometimes can seem as though charm counts as much as credentials. All this can lead to job-hunting paralysis.

Here's the solution: realize that doubts about your candidacy are normal and focus instead on all the positives you offer. Also remember that rejection in a job search is not a comment on your worth as a person. It simply means that a wide range of factors, many of which were beyond your control, didn't fall into place to make you the right person for the job. Rather than internalizing the rejection and letting it slow you down, accept it and move on to the next iron in the fire.

Getting Ahead in Your Career and Job

Employers don't hire people just to fill up square footage in the office or the factory (or wherever the work takes place). They want employees who don't merely go through the motions of doing a job but who go the extra mile to bring an innovative, efficient, problem-solving approach to improving the organization's bottom line. They want people who can help them not just compete with, but also outsmart and outpace, their competitors.

Making the effort to make a difference is not only good for your employer; you benefit as well. When you stretch the limits of your abilities and see achievements beyond the basics of what your job requires, you become more marketable. Then, when you set out to land your next job and the one after that, you'll have an impressive track record of accomplishments to discuss on your résumé, in cover letters, in interviews, and when negotiating salary and other terms of a deal.

Unfortunately, most people get so caught up in the day-to-day demands of their jobs and in more pressing matters that they don't make the time to look at what's going on beyond their cubicle walls. If you put off looking at the big picture of your career and your professional community or industry, you may come to regret that procrastination down the road. If you don't see how you'll find the time to go that extra mile, consider these simple things you can do:

- **Be visible.** Become involved in your professional community at large, not only by joining professional and trade associations and reading the newsletter, but by participating in these organizations. Attend meetings and seminars, help coordinate events, write for their publications, comment on their blog, and even run for office. Schedule a minimum of one activity per month.

- **Network.** To stay informed about developments in your profession or industry as a whole, and to connect with people who could help you out in your career down the road, make a point of getting together with people outside of your own company. Schedule breakfast or lunch meetings, keep in touch by phone and email, expand the size of your online networks, post status updates and comments on LinkedIn and Facebook, build a following on Twitter, or connect in any way that's feasible.

- **Keep your skills sharp.** Take stock of areas where you could use some improvement. Examples include public speaking, making presentations, working on teams, managing people, project management, oral or written communication, and sales.

YOU'RE NOT ALONE

On my last job, I focused so much on the needs of my clients and on getting my projects done perfectly, that I forgot I am my number-one client. I should always keep in mind that my most important project is advancing in my career.

—Avery B., sales manager

You may be tempted to say, "But I don't have time to do those things." I know it might seem like a reach, but making those objectives a priority will save you time in the long run and is therefore worth every minute you'll have to spend on it. Never put off your career future.

Academia: A Procrastination Breeding Ground

Whether you're in high school, college, graduate school, or a working adult taking part-time courses, your life as a student is likely to be brimming with potential distractions and psychological ups and downs. The remaining sections of this chapter look at what some of those procrastination catalysts are and how they can be kept at bay, with a focus on issues unique to each level of education: high school, college, and graduate studies; issues of older adults returning to school are covered as well.

Procrastination in High School

Bad habits related to doing homework, studying for exams, and writing papers usually start in high school, if not earlier. Sometimes, procrastination starts because your home environment isn't conducive to studying. You also might find yourself too loaded down with household chores and family obligations, or with sports or other extracurriculars to have time for schoolwork. Other homes have the opposite problem, with parents who go overboard in pressuring their kids to excel at school, thus making them rebel or feel overwhelmed and fearful of failure.

Maybe your procrastination comes from inside. You may have a learning disability or attention deficit problem that makes it difficult to prioritize your time, stay focused, and complete your reading or writing. Or maybe you've just never learned good study habits.

If you're a high school student who finds yourself cramming for exams at the last minute, starting papers and projects the night before they're due, or always feeling behind, here are some things you can do to be more effective:

- Don't give in to all-or-nothing thinking. Instead of leaving all your studying or writing until the last minute and having to spend a whole evening or weekend getting it done, try to break up the project into smaller parts and start earlier. Use the chip-away technique described in Chapter 8 to get things done little by little.

- Keep your family in the loop. As soon as you find out when big projects or papers are due or when quizzes or exams will be given, let your parents or guardians know. That way, they can plan family activities and outings around those dates to avoid conflicts with times you need to be studying.

- Don't load up on extracurricular activities just because you think that's the only way to get into a good college. Good grades and recommendations from teachers are just as important for college applications, so don't get your schedule so packed with activities that you can't keep up with academics.

- If your home environment is not conducive to studying, study at school or a library whenever possible. Try to schedule two or three specific times per week when you go to that study spot (or even do it every day!). Consider it an appointment that is firm and as much a part of your routine as your sports practice, music lessons, or anything else.

- If your parents are putting too much pressure on you to excel at school, and you find yourself procrastinating as a way to rebel or because you feel overwhelmed, talk to them about what you're feeling. If they won't listen, talk to a teacher or counselor.

- If you seem to have more difficulty organizing your time or getting your work done than your friends do, talk to your parents (or a teacher or guidance counselor) about the problem. Ask them if they think you should be tested for learning disabilities or an attention disorder.

- If learning difficulties aren't the issue, but you still have trouble getting your work done and organizing your studies, ask your parents about hiring a private tutor for you, or see if your school offers free or low-cost study skills help.

- Close the screens! Shut off your phone, your computer (unless you have to use it for homework), and the TV. Your friends will still be on Facebook and Tumblr when you are finished with your work and ready to get back on.

If you kick the procrastination habit now, while you're still in high school—or keep yourself from developing the habit in the first place—you'll be much better off down the road as you continue your education.

Procrastination in College

If you had been a fly on the ivy-covered wall during my senior year in college, you'd never have believed that I could turn out to be an ex-procrastinator later in life. There I was in the final semester, taking five classes and two independent studies at once, rushing to complete papers, and cramming for exams in order to meet my degree requirements. All this work was due to the fact that I had spent much of my college career dropping courses I didn't like or taking incompletes in ones I had slept through. (How dare they hold classes before noon?!) For three and a half years, I told myself that I would catch up later. I paid for that procrastination by having a stressful, overloaded final semester while most of my classmates were taking it easy, coasting toward graduation.

It's so easy to procrastinate in college. You have the distractions of extracurricular activities and a social life, plus roommates in dorms or apartments tempting you with fun things to do. You have semester-long projects with faraway deadlines and no one watching over you to make sure you work steadily toward those deadlines. Then you have the pressure of getting good grades, fulfilling requirements, and making sure the tuition is paid. Based on extensive research, social scientists estimate that as much as 90 percent of students on any given campus procrastinate. Most studies have found that writing papers is the biggest area of procrastination, followed by studying for tests and doing homework.

If you're a commuter student, you might be working full or part time and going to college part time, so you have the added demands of a job, which can make it hard to keep schoolwork a priority.

> **YOU'RE NOT ALONE**
>
> When I was a university student in England, cleaning out the bathroom was a chore I avoided as much as possible. The nearer we got to final exams, however, the cleaner that bathroom got. I'd ask myself, "Shall I study or do more household chores? Hmm, the kitchen and TV room are spotless, I'll go clean the bathroom."
>
> —Tanya W., corporate treasury manager

The strategies that work for overcoming procrastination in college are the same ones that help in any other type of situation. If you're a college student struggling with procrastination, be sure to read Chapter 8, if you haven't done so already. Also, keep these points in mind:

- Don't get caught up in the culture of procrastination. Think about how silly it is to brag about being far behind or having to cram for an exam at the last minute. There are plenty of other ways to be one of the gang and to interact with your classmates without having to pull all-nighters.

- Realize that the adrenaline rush you get from doing work at the last minute may feel good now, but eleventh-hour cramming gets harder to pull off later in life. If you come to rely on the habit now, you'll have a hard time kicking it later.

- Although internships, other work experiences, community service, and campus activities are important for a well-rounded college experience, keep your schedule manageable by not taking on too much in any one semester or academic year. College is a time to learn and have fun, not a time to burn out.

MATTER OF FACT

If you tend to be motivated by money and are having trouble overcoming procrastination in college or have been putting off going to college, let this fact from recent years' findings by the Bureau of Labor Statistics motivate you:

Annual earnings of college graduates are nearly twice that of high school graduates and two and a half times that of high school dropouts.

If you follow these suggestions, you'll have more time for fun or whatever else it is you want to do besides study.

Procrastination in Graduate School

If my own experience is at all typical, procrastination is often less of a problem once you reach graduate school, even if you were a big procrastinator in college (until you get to the thesis or dissertation stage, that is!). Most grad students have reasonably clear career goals or a love of a particular academic subject, which motivates them to work toward an advanced degree. Their classes tend to be small, and faculty advisors are involved in their lives, so they have a built-in support system.

Graduate students also tend to be more mature and responsible and less distracted by social lives and extensive extracurricular activities than their undergrad counterparts.

But before I give too rosy a picture of graduate school, let's remember what procrastination is: it's a habit. No matter how favorable the conditions are for productivity, someone who suffers from the procrastination habit is going to find ways to put off things, even in grad school.

ACTION TACTIC

Many graduate students don't finish theses or dissertations because when they move away from campus after completing coursework, they become isolated and removed from academic life. If you're trying to write your final project from a distance, be sure to stay in the loop by having regular phone meetings or Skype sessions with your advisor and staying in touch with your classmates and faculty.

As a graduate student, you are more likely than an undergrad to feel divided between two worlds: the academic world and real life. You may have a burgeoning professional career requiring time, energy, and attention, and possibly a family that demands the same.

What's the solution? The key lies in taking stock of your commitments in your various life roles and making sure that your expectations, and those of your bosses, professors, and family, are realistic.

QUICKSAND!

There's more to schoolwork than papers and exams. Keeping on top of academic red tape is important for procrastinators, who might let problems go unresolved until serious consequences develop. Make sure you watch out for deadlines related to financial aid, tuition and fees, course incompletes, and transcript discrepancies.

Returning to School Before the Twelfth of Never

Gone are the days when college campuses were populated by nothing but 18- to 24-year-old students. Now, you're likely to see more than a few gray hairs among the jeans and backpacks. Adults age 25 and up are going back to school in record numbers—for the college degrees they never earned when they were younger, for graduate degrees, or just for individual courses. They're also more likely to be doing it virtually—rarely, if ever, setting foot on a campus.

Returning to school does wonders for your career advancement, income potential, and self-confidence. Plus, you learn interesting stuff. So what's keeping you from doing it? See whether any of these excuses ring a bell:

"I won't fit in with all those younger students."

Reality: It's very unlikely that you'll be the only returning student, particularly if you select a school or program that encourages adult learners.

"I don't feel as smart as I used to. My memory is shot."

Reality: Sure, you may have spent a few more brain cells than the perky 19-year-old next to you in class, but that doesn't mean you can't learn. Your maturity, life experience, and genuine desire to learn (three things that 19-year-old may not have) will make up for any cellular breakdown.

"I don't have time to go back to school."

Reality: If you make it a priority, you will have time for it. Many returning students juggle school with job and family responsibilities. See where you could make some adjustments to allow school to take a more prominent place in your life.

"I can't afford it."

Reality: You'd be amazed how many sources of financial aid are out there. It just takes advance planning and persistent research to uncover the options and apply for them. Some colleges will let you speak with a financial aid advisor before you're even admitted so you can get a head start on budgeting and applying for loans, grants, scholarships, and fellowships.

"My grades and standardized test scores were lousy when I was last in school, so I'll never get in anywhere."

Reality: If you've been out of high school or college for several years or more, most admissions officers will be more interested in what you've done recently than in your ancient history. They take your work and life experience into account and usually assume that you're more mature, responsible, and motivated now than you were then.

If you have difficulty accepting any of those realities, don't just take my word for it. Contact the schools you're considering attending and ask whether they can put you in touch with any current students around your age or any who have life circumstances in common with you (such as working full time or being a parent). Talk to the students about the pros and cons of being a returning student. You might learn that, even though it's a struggle, being back in school gives them a sense of accomplishment and career opportunities that they never could have had without further education.

The Least You Need to Know

- Putting off career decisions limits your potential for growth, satisfaction, and earnings.
- Putting off looking for a job is often due to a lack of a clear job target or search strategy or to fears and self-doubt.
- The procrastination habit often develops during high school and continues in college due to the distractions of social life and extracurricular activities.
- The close-knit community of students and faculty in graduate school makes it easier to overcome procrastination.

Procrastination in Your Tech Life

Chapter 13

In This Chapter

- The cold, hard facts about why technology causes us to procrastinate
- Keeping gadgets, games, and online gizmos from taking over your life
- Preventing email from growing like weeds

Here's a riddle: How many checks of Facebook, viewings of YouTube videos, and browsing of online beach house rentals does it take to write a chapter in a book on procrastination? Answer: Many more than your humble author cares to admit. The distractions technology provides are almost irresistible, even for an expert on overcoming procrastination.

The very machines we use to do our real work on a daily basis are gateways to a world of really interesting stuff. In a matter of seconds, we can peek into the lives of our friends around the globe through Facebook, Tumblr, Twitter, and countless other social networks. In the course of a day we might receive more email messages than a whole neighborhood's worth of physical mailboxes could hold in a month. And when work tasks or personal chores seem undesirable, we turn to fun and games on our computers or phones to while away the time.

We also put off dealing with the technology itself. How long has it been since you backed up your files? Cleared the icon clutter off your desktop? Emptied your email inbox? Vacuumed your keyboard? Posted to your blog? Updated your LinkedIn profile?

How many items are languishing on your backburner technology to-do list—dealing with wiring, cabling, or networking, converting audio or video tapes to digital, scanning and organizing photos, replacing your fading printer cartridge?

Whether technology is the cause of procrastination in other areas of your life or is the thing you procrastinate about, this chapter offers solutions for regaining control of your time without having to become a Luddite.

Understanding Technology Procrastination Through Statistics

In Chapter 2, you learned about external factors that can lead to procrastination. You know that procrastination comes not only from the psychological games we play to tell ourselves we can put something off; it also results from factors around us that provide distractions, temptations, or unfavorable conditions and, therefore, foster procrastination. We might not put away clean laundry for days because our closet or drawers are too stuffed. We might not get all we need to get done at work because our workspace is uncomfortable or disorganized. We might put off household chores when a procrastination-enabling friend lures us away with something more fun to do.

MATTER OF FACT

A Luddite is someone who opposes industrial change and innovation. The term has come to mean anyone who is very low-tech. It's your relative who doesn't do email or whose phone has no data plan, only voice calling—or maybe they have no mobile phone at all! It's the friend you can't entice to join Facebook, who only wants to talk to you on the phone. The term's origins lie in bands of textile workers in early 1800s England who rioted and destroyed industrial machinery for fear that it would take away jobs.

Now, take those and many other routine factors of daily life—our "bricks and mortar" life—and multiply them exponentially to come up with the people, places, and things of our tech life that can influence procrastination. Instead of having one or two roommates or a few family members in your home who might coax you to neglect your to-do list, you have hundreds, maybe even thousands, of friends and contacts a click away in your social networks. Or instead of having some disorganized papers and scattered post-it notes on your physical desk that cause you to put off tackling a report, you might have hundreds of megabytes of computer clutter holding you back.

These are only a couple of the myriad examples of ways that technology—hardware, software, mobile devices, applications, games, the internet, email, and more—have become one of the most significant causes of procrastinating behavior, as well as a category of things we procrastinate about.

The statistics offered in the following sections show the staggering scope of your tech life and the impact it could be having on you. Keep in mind that by the time this book gets into your hands (or the e-book version gets onto your screen!), whether that's only months or several years from the time of this writing, many of these figures will have grown to even more astonishing levels.

Internet Usage Statistics

The following statistics help us see what we're up against as we try to get things done in this digital age.

- Nearly 250 billion emails are sent every day. (Email Marketing Benchmark Report, 2012)

- Individuals and businesses maintained almost 367 million websites. (Netcraft, 2012)

- There were 152 million blogs on the internet in 2012, as tracked by BlogPulse.

- At the time of its filing for an initial public offering in February 2012, Facebook had 845 million active users.

- Over 201 billion videos were watched per month on YouTube and more than 2 billion per month on Facebook, with the average internet user in the United States watching 186 online videos per month. (Pingdom, 2011)

- Four and a half million photos were uploaded to Flickr each day and an estimated 100 billion photos were hosted on Facebook in 2011. (Pingdom, 2012)

According to Twitter's own record-keeping in 2011, we spent a lot of time using their social network and microblogging service:

- Twitter users sent 140 million Tweets per day in just one month.

- To get from the very first Tweet to the billionth Tweet took only three years, two months, and one day.

- By 2011, a billion Tweets were being sent every week.

If you find yourself being sucked into the web, often at the expense of other things you should be doing, you are certainly not alone!

QUICKSAND!

Watch out for procrastination enablers and negative online peer pressure. You really can ignore or decline Farmville invitations and tell friends you can't play their word games.

Statistics on Mobile Phones and Tablet Devices

These days, distractions follow us wherever we go. With our mobile technology and tablet computers, we can stay plugged in at all times. While this reality can be great for keeping up with our work or managing our busy personal lives, these same devices can pull us in not-so-productive directions. The vast majority of us in the developed world are subjected to the challenge of balancing these tools for efficiency with a healthy balance of fun, but may find ourselves feeling like slaves to them.

- There are 6 billion cell phone subscriptions worldwide and 1.2 billion mobile web usage subscriptions. (MobiThinking. com, 2012)

- More than 300 million smart phones were sold in 2010, and in just one quarter of 2011 the top 10 smart phone manufacturers (such as Nokia, Apple, and Samsung) sold nearly 110 million units. (MobiThinking.com, 2012)

- Portio Research found that almost 7 trillion text messages were sent worldwide in 2010 and predicted the number to hit 8 trillion in 2011.

- According to the Pew Internet and Mobile Life Project (www.pewinternet.org), text messaging users in 2011 sent or received an average of 41.5 messages per day. But when 18- to 24-year-olds were singled out, they were found to send or receive an average of 109.5 text messages per day!

- Mobile users of Twitter increased 182 percent from 2010 to 2011. (@Twitter.com)

- As of the end of 2011, Facebook was accessed through mobile devices by 350 million users, and those who used Facebook on the go were twice as active on the site as nonmobile users. (MobiThinking.com, 2012)

- Forrester Research, Inc., predicts that by 2015, sales of tablet computers will reach 195 million.

ACTION TACTIC

If you find yourself particularly prone to procrastination at work, step back and examine how you feel about your job or the business you're in. Are you bored? Overloaded? Losing interest? Under-challenged or over-challenged? You might have to deal with these issues before you can expect strategies for overcoming procrastination to work.

Games, Shopping, and Other Diversions by the Numbers

In the course of a busy workday or a day of household chores and personal to-do items, we access the internet for plenty of legitimate reasons. We instant message our colleagues to collaborate on work projects. We text our teenagers to hunt them down. We make purchases in much less time than it would take to go to the mall. We book travel, get driving directions, make dining reservations, check the weather without having to sit through 25 minutes of television news, and pass the time in long lines with a quick game on our phone. There's nothing wrong with all that.

The problem comes in when time spent online playing games, shopping, reading the news, or with other diversions starts to consume too much of our time and attention, at the expense of other things we need to be accomplishing.

- Customers were forecasted to buy and sell $8 billion of merchandise on eBay in 2012.

- In July 2010 Amazon CEO Jeff Bezos reported that $1 billion in products were ordered from his site in the prior 12 months on mobile devices.

- Localytics reported in 2010 that one in four downloaded mobile apps is never used again.

- According to Neilsen 2010 findings, the most popular categories of apps used on mobile devices were games, news, maps, social networking, and music. Facebook, Google Maps, and The Weather Channel were the most used—not just downloaded but actually used—apps on mobile devices.

- More than 300,000 mobile apps were developed from 2008 to 2011, with 10.9 billion downloads. (MobiThinking, 2012)

- Facebook reports that in 2011 an online poker site was the most popular page on Facebook, beating out the pages for Justin Bieber, Katy Perry, and the Farmville Cows.

With all these fun things to do that are so conveniently at our fingertips, who has time to work or take out the trash or take care of such silliness as reaching life goals?

QUICKSAND!

Technology market research firm Radicati Group estimates that up to 90 percent of email sent worldwide is spam or viruses. Recipient, beware!

Key Changes to Make in Your Tech Life to Start Reining It In

Email is one of the biggest hurdles in our technology-drenched lives, so that topic gets its own section, "Strategies for Taming Email and Reclaiming Your Inbox," later in this chapter. Meanwhile, in the following sections are tips for dealing with many aspects of technology that we put off handling or that cause us to procrastinate in other areas of life.

Keep Electronic Clutter at Bay

When our physical surroundings become cluttered, the problem is obvious. You have to clear a path to get into a room or are unable to close a closet door because of all the objects spilling out. But our electronic, or digital, clutter is not nearly as obvious, so it can easily sneak up and end up slowing us down.

To get rid of clutter in your tech life and to prevent it from building back up, make these some rules to live by:

- Stop acquiring unnecessary stuff—extra computers, peripherals, software, gaming devices, anything at all that you don't need more of. That nice sales associate at Best Buy will get along without you just fine.

- Don't download every app that comes along. You already saw in earlier statistics that many downloaded apps are never used again. Before you get it, even if it's free, make sure you really need it and will use it.

- Donate, recycle, or resell your old computers, peripherals, and phones. Be brutally honest with yourself about whether you will ever use them again, and if the answer is no, get rid of them.

- If you scan papers, find a place to file them right away on your hard drive or external storage drive. Don't leave the files randomly strewn across your desktop. Set up a system of folders and file them accordingly.

- Consolidate your digital photos into one site or in one of your own storage drives if not keeping them online. Over the years, many photography sites have cropped up, and you might have tried them all out. This results in photo albums scattered throughout cyberspace. Track them down and put them into one place so that when you need to get your hands on a photo to show someone or to print, you know where it is.

QUICKSAND!

Before downloading yet another mobile application, make sure you are really going to use it and that using it is a worthwhile way to spend your time. According to Localytics, one in four mobile apps is downloaded but never used again.

Avoid Technology Distractions

You might not have an electronic clutter problem—or might be taking care of it soon—but procrastination can still arise from giving into the distractions in our tech lives. Try these strategies for staying on the straight and narrow, while still having some fun.

- Consider scheduling times in your day or throughout the week that are dedicated to the activities you are most likely to be distracted by, whether that's reading the news, playing games, or checking into your social networks.

- If you don't schedule blocks of time for diversions, then at least give yourself time limits. Some people can pop onto Facebook, do a 20-second scan of their newsfeed, post a quick status update, and sign off to get back to work. Others end up being sucked into following every posted link, studying every photo, looking up yet another set of long-lost friends, and finding that they've lost an hour of their lives. You know which kind you are. Limit yourself accordingly. Set a timer if you have to!

- If you have more than one computer or a computer plus a tablet, try to designate one for work (or personal/household business if you don't have a job outside of home) and one for goofing off, and maybe even keep them in different rooms. You'll be less likely to toggle back and forth between playing Angry Birds and answering email from your angry boss.

ACTION TACTIC

Before going on vacation or leaving for business travel, block some time in your calendar shortly after your return to catch up on email and clear out your box.

- If you don't have more than one computing device, or it isn't feasible to separate work and play in terms of hardware, then set up separate user accounts for yourself on the same machine. At least you'll have the hurdle of logging out of one account and into another, and that might cause you to pause and think about whether you really should be playing or working.

- If games are your downfall to the point that they become a vice instead of a harmless, brief diversion, then try playing only on a gaming machine with your TV rather than on your phone or computer.

- Consider blocking sites that cause you to procrastinate too much. Parental controls don't have to be just for minors—parent yourself!

- Turn off instant messaging (IM). Whether you disconnect all the time or only temporarily, you'll cut back on interruptions that break your momentum and concentration. You can also do this only on certain sites. Maybe you aren't allowed to disconnect from Microsoft Office Communicator at work, but you can appear invisible to friends and family trying to chat you up on Gmail.

- Limit the number of social networks you belong to. Keep in mind how much time each one takes up in your life and how your time-wasting is multiplied when you participate actively or frequently browse multiple sites. I'm not saying social networks are a waste of time—far from it—but when you spread yourself too thin across too many sites, you're increasing your distractions exponentially.

QUICKSAND!

Are your online activities causing you to lose sleep? Being tired can make you more prone to procrastinating behavior, so think twice before you stay up until the wee hours putting one more image on Pinterest, streaming yet another TV episode on Hulu, or Googling more old classmates.

Manage Your Time Online and Onscreen

Even after placing limits on the digital culprits that distract you—or maybe you aren't one to succumb to all that nonsense in the first place—you are likely still to face challenges dealing with how you spend your time online or on your computers and phones in general. Consider these tips:

- Streamline your online calendars into only one calendar, if possible. Share online calendars with family members or work colleagues.

- If you're considering starting a blog or a fan/business page on a site like Facebook, think long and hard about whether you have enough time to devote to it. Only start one if you know you can post regularly to it, communicate promptly with fans or members, and generally keep it fresh and interesting.

- If you already have a blog, website, or fan page and struggle to keep up with it, schedule regular times in your calendar to devote to it on a daily, weekly, or less frequent basis depending on the nature of the site. Treat these times as a firm appointment you cannot miss.

- When appropriate, delegate website updates—even blog posts, with your input—to someone else if your time is very limited.

- Step away from all "screens" occasionally. Go low-tech for a while with no email, no computer use, no television, no gaming devices, maybe even no phone if you don't need to be reached for emergency purposes. Read a book, write a letter, plant some flowers, go for a walk (even try it without music in your ears!). You might not be able to do this every day or even every week, but set some time periodically and regularly to unplug.

YOU'RE NOT ALONE

Do you ever worry that your time spent online is over the top? Have friends or family members expressed concern that you spend too much time on the internet, or has your work or personal life suffered seriously because of your online activities?

Internet addiction, first presented as a serious research topic by Dr. Kimberly Young at the American Psychological Association's national conference in 1996, shares many of the symptoms, negative life impact, and recommended treatment solutions as other more common addictions and impulsive behavior. A national study conducted by a team from Stanford University's School of Medicine estimated that nearly one in eight Americans suffers from at least one sign of problematic internet use. For more information and helpful resources, visit The Center for Internet Addiction at www.netaddiction.com.

- Use low-tech methods on occasion to get your work done or to regain momentum when you're getting stuck and feel procrastination creeping in. Step away from the computer, get out of your desk chair, put paper and pen in hand, and curl up in a comfy chair (but don't fall asleep!). Dry-erase boards (not online boards!) are also a nice alternative that can get the intellectual and creative juices flowing.

- Watch the multitasking. As an avid multitasker myself, I'd be a hypocrite if I told you never to do it. But if you're reading this book, you probably are at risk for procrastinating when you jump from task to task. And our tech lives make this even more of a challenge since we can so easily hop onto a social network, game, the news, email, or other distractors while we're supposed to be doing something else. Force yourself to stick with one focus at a time.

Give some thought to which of the previous strategies are relevant to you and your issues. Be honest with yourself about where you could shave some time spent online and increase your efficiencies. That doesn't mean you can't take a break now and then to indulge in some fun online, but just try to learn to do so as a reward for, or to recharge yourself for, getting things done in life.

YOU'RE NOT ALONE

Running a busy consulting practice, I have to make sure that reading and responding to email doesn't take up too much of my time. I've developed some rules for myself that work well:

- Email does not download into my inbox automatically and all notifications are turned off.
- I download email two times per day, at 11 A.M. and 4 P.M. (Not downloading email first thing in the morning is my key to better productivity.)
- I only read an email *once* and deal with its needs right then.
- Regarding e-newsletters, if I am not getting anything out of one after receiving three issues, I unsubscribe.

I admit that I go through spells of sticking to my rules and then cheating on my rules, but I always come back to them and am glad I did.

—Leslie Kuban, franchise consultant, FranNet of Georgia

Strategies for Taming Email and Reclaiming Your Inbox

When was the last time your work or personal email inbox was empty? How about your inboxes on Facebook, LinkedIn, your blog, or other sites? How many email messages are waiting for a reply from you? Do you compulsively check email on your phone when you should be doing other things?

Email can be both a distraction that causes us to procrastinate— though a necessary distraction, usually—and something we procrastinate about. We put off deleting email we don't need to keep, filing email we do need to save, answering email that requires a response, or taking action on email that adds to our task list. We also might be slow to take care of projects because our inboxes get so crowded that we can't find important email that relates to the project.

To preserve the real purpose of email—an efficient, convenient way to communicate—and keep it from slowing you down or causing unnecessary anxiety, use these strategies:

- Minimize what comes in. Unsubscribe to email you never asked for in the first place. Get off of distribution lists. Either don't sign on for, or check the boxes to opt out of, email alerts and updates that various sites offer. Politely decline e-newsletters you don't end up reading. Be careful about giving out your email address.

- Consider setting up a separate email address for your online purchases and other nonserious online activity. When you give out your email address to sign up for a free (or paid) membership on a site, you're going to end up with mail that might not be very critical. And when you make purchases online, use this dedicated address so that future mail from that company doesn't clog up your main mailbox.

- If an email is obviously junk, delete it without reading it. Like rubbernecking when driving past a bad car accident, it can be tempting to read junk mail just because you are so amazed at how stupid it is.

- Try answering most email right away if it's a fairly simple matter. This takes nothing more than sheer determination to stop the voices in your head that are saying, "Oh, I can deal with that later."

- Set up a process for dealing with more complicated email responses. First, shoot off a quick reply to let the sender know you got the message (if a read receipt wasn't sent). Then, file the email in a folder you keep for mail to respond to at a later time. Next, make sure your calendar is marked with a specific block of time you will be dealing with the pending mail in that folder, whether that's multiple times throughout a day, once a day, or less often.

- Create an automatic reply to go out during times when you know you won't be able to respond to email quickly. Let people know you are in a full day of meetings, or traveling, or are working on a special project.

- Delegate email responses whenever possible. Take a careful look at your work responsibilities and see if you've been handling things that should be taken care of by someone else. Or if it's personal mail, partner with your so-called partners—spouse or significant other, other family members, friends you're involved in projects with, etc., to see if you can divide and conquer email.

- Report spam to your company's IT department or to your Internet Service Provider or social network administrators so that you can help stem the flow of future junk mail and viruses.

- Set up a simple but highly functional filing system for your email. If you don't already have a set of folders that you can move email into when you need to save it, set one up. If you already have one, make sure the categories are working for you.

- Get your inbox to empty. This might take some time if you have hundreds (Or is it thousands? Dare I ask?) of messages languishing in your mailbox. Set aside a big block of time, or multiple blocks of time, on a quiet day when you're not likely to have email coming in as fast as you clear it out. Force yourself to work swiftly and without mercy as you delete, give quick replies to, or file each piece of mail until you get to the magic number of zero.

- Keep bringing your inbox down to empty on a regular basis. Depending on how much mail you typically receive and how busy your days are, determine if it's more realistic to get your box to zero once a day, once a week, or once every couple of weeks. Schedule time in your calendar—a fixed appointment you take seriously—to devote to clearing out your box.

- Don't use your inbox as a task list. This only creates inbox clutter. If you need to take action on an email, or if an email provides information you need to complete a project, don't let it sit in your inbox. Make note of the action in your to-do list and then file the email in a folder you've set up for that project.

- To avoid being distracted by email, consider turning off visible or audible alerts, notifications, and previews that cause you to be compulsive about checking email when you're in the midst of other things.

ACTION TACTIC

Instead of focusing only on managing your email inbox, be sure to keep your folders of sent and deleted messages under control as well. In some email systems, when those folders get overloaded, your inbox shuts down and won't send or receive messages. You then end up having extra work to do to resend messages you thought were on their way or to contact people who were trying to reach you. Avoid this by periodically emptying your sent and deleted folders.

By employing these strategies for taming the inbox beast, you can keep email from running your life!

The Least You Need to Know

- The volume of email, texting, mobile phone apps, and internet usage that is a regular part of most people's lives is overwhelming and contributes to procrastinating behavior.

- Just as with your physical surroundings, your electronic or digital life needs to be uncluttered in order to free yourself up to take action.

- Managing your time online and with technology in general requires removing your most problematic distractions and setting time limits or schedules.

- Your email box can get empty and remain at a manageable level if you reduce the amount of email coming in and employ strategies for answering, filing, and deleting mail in a timely manner.

Making Procrastination a Thing of the Past

In This Chapter

- Staying motivated long after you close this book
- Identifying your procrastination hot spots to keep them from flaring up again
- Sorting out your priorities and values
- Making the commitment to change

Unless you've skipped ahead to this chapter (hey, there's no law against it), then you've come a long way. You've learned why you procrastinate and why it's so important to stop doing so. You've seen what it takes to become an ex-procrastinator: understand the change process, find support from other people, get organized, and make good decisions. You've also found out that any urge to procrastinate can be overcome by doing three simple things: stop, look, and listen. And you've learned that once you squash the urge, you can use the 10 techniques described in Chapter 8 to start taking action in the specific ways suggested in Chapters 9 through 13.

I hope that, at this point, you've already started to break the procrastination habit and are seeing some changes in your approach to life, even if they're only minor ones for now. If not, then I hope, at least, that you're now motivated to do something about your problems. I want you to have not only a fire in your belly but a strategy in mind.

Seven Simple Rules for Putting Off Procrastination

If you remember nothing else from this book, remember these seven themes for success in overcoming procrastination:

1. Change will occur only if you give yourself a reality check about your procrastination habit, commit to breaking it, and stay that way.

2. Productivity is enhanced by having a balanced life, one in which you get things done but have fun and relax as well.

3. To know what to do on a day-to-day basis—that is, what your priorities are—you have to know what your overall life values are. You also have to understand the difference between values and priorities.

4. Shed your old identity. Just because everyone around you has come to know you as a procrastinator, and you've internalized their view, don't get stuck with that label.

5. Use the techniques. Just reading this book doesn't mean that you will automatically start using the stop, look, and listen solution or any of the other strategies for taking action. It takes sheer determination to get yourself to pause long enough to become aware that you are on the brink of procrastinating and to do something about it.

6. Keeping clutter from re-accumulating is more important than you might think; it's a key to staying organized and being productive.

7. Admit when you need help. If you are having difficulty taking control of your behavior and using the action strategies, or if you need some help understanding the strategies better, then you have to be willing to get some help. Whether you turn to a support team of family and friends or an expert, connecting with real, live human beings is essential for making the strategies work.

YOU'RE NOT ALONE

We only become what we are by the radical and deep-seeded refusal of that which others have made us.

—Jean-Paul Sartre, twentieth-century French philosopher and writer

These seven rules, together with a genuine desire to stop procrastinating, get things done, and reach your goals, will make it happen.

Make Balance a Priority

I know it's easier said than done, but even if you make just a little effort toward keeping some balance in your life, you might be surprised by the positive changes that result. The best way to do this is to keep in mind that balance is not achieved by a mechanical process. It's not a matter of scheduling times into your daily planner to take a walk in the park, meditate or pray, go to the zoo with a child, do something artistic, or just sit and do nothing. It's more of a mindset. It's understanding what the best ways are for you to nourish your mind, body, and soul.

QUICKSAND!

Don't forget that you have to look at your to-do lists on a regular basis, schedule times to do the things on them, and follow your schedule. Setting up these organizational systems is only the first step. If you ignore them, they won't work.

While no one has cornered the market on the secret to having a perfectly balanced life—I certainly haven't (but I keep trying)—there are typically three main keys to having a balanced life:

- **Have fun.** Do things you enjoy while still meeting your responsibilities.

- **Be grateful.** Make a conscious effort to think about, and be thankful for, what's good in your life. Even the busiest person, who claims not to have time to lead a more balanced life because of work, school, or family demands, can take a minute to do this.

- **Connect.** Connect with the things you do and the people around you instead of just going through the motions.

By the way, there's nothing inherently wrong with scheduling balance into your calendar, if that's the only way to ensure that you'll start making the time to have fun, be grateful, and connect. But true balance is a frame of mind, not an appointment.

Value Your Priorities and Prioritize Your Values

Ultimately, being a more effective, efficient, and accomplished (and, yes, balanced) person becomes an issue of working in harmony with your values and keeping your priorities straight. "Gee, umm, that sounds good ... I guess ... but what does it mean?" you might ask. Allow me to illustrate the point by sharing one last personal example with you. This example comes from an experience I had while writing the first edition of this book more than 10 years ago, but the lessons learned from it are relevant today and still guide my day-to-day actions.

For several decades, a question has been woven into the fabric of American popular culture (at least for those of us old enough to have been born when this happened): Where were you when John F. Kennedy was shot? Unfortunately, a new question related to the same family was added in the late 1990s: Where were you when you heard that the plane flown by JFK Jr. was missing and that he and his wife and sister-in-law had died? While not a crisis on the massive scale that 9/11 would be a few years later, the JFK Jr. tragedy resonated around the world at the time, and particularly in my little world.

I know where I was. It was a steamy July weekend, and I was at home in New York about to get back to writing this chapter for the first edition of this book, just days from my final deadline. In addition to the sadness I felt over the loss of promising, productive young people, I began to have the sort of thoughts that many people have when faced with a reminder of how fragile our lives are.

My first thought was that I need to treasure my family and friends like never before because they might not be here tomorrow. My next thought was that I need to live each day to the fullest, accomplishing my goals while I still can because I might not be here tomorrow.

My daughter and my work are among my top values, so those thoughts were nothing new. But when mortality slaps you in the face, especially when it's the death of three people who are close to your own age, the importance of those values is magnified to the nth degree.

 YOU'RE NOT ALONE

It seems that the older I get, the more my priorities change, and some tasks end up on hold longer. My house was once one of my main concerns. Now, I don't redecorate as often. I value more spending time with people I love and care for.

—Judy T., homemaker, grandmother, and co-owner/manager of a Texas cattle ranch

Back down on Earth, I looked at my to-do list for that weekend:

- Wrap up two near-finished chapters of the book
- Write a draft of an article for *The New York Times*
- Research hotels to make reservations for a vacation
- Buy a birthday gift for a friend
- Go to the gym
- Grocery shop

Before I woke up to the shocking news of the plane crash, I had planned to spend the entire weekend at the computer, cranking out chapters and an article as fast as I could. My daughter, who was very young at the time, was going to be out with her father visiting some of our friends. The idea was that he would keep her "out of my hair" so that I could get some work done, given that my deadlines for two writing projects were approaching so quickly.

Okay, so that plan fit with my work value: Reach your goals while you can because you might not live to see tomorrow (and because you enjoy the work). But what about the other value of treasuring loved ones? It looked like I was facing a conflict of values. What good would it do to have a book finished and an article published in a big-deal paper if my child was away from me that day and something happened and well … I don't even want to think about it. On the other hand, I couldn't abandon my responsibilities and quit doing work and just sit around and hug her all the time. What's the solution?

The answer lies in realizing that values and priorities are not the same thing. I thought I was facing a values conflict that weekend, but I wasn't. I was facing a question of how to prioritize my time in alignment with my values.

That weekend, working had to be a priority. Sure, I could've said to hell with it and spent both days playing with my family. But there's a time and a place for that sort of semi-reckless abandon. That weekend was not one of those. By choosing to work, I was not saying that my work was more important than my family. I was recognizing that work had to be a priority that weekend. I was acknowledging that not meeting my professional obligations would end up having serious negative consequences—not just for myself and my career, but for the people on the other end of my work who were counting on me.

So there you have it. I wouldn't let myself feel guilty, because that wouldn't do anyone any good. Instead, I finished my writing, despite having one eye and ear focused on the round-the-clock television news (just as my parents had been glued to the television watching the news of JFK's death when I was a toddler). I also managed to squeeze in a quick workout and to pick up a birthday gift at the bookstore next to the gym. I delegated the grocery shopping to my husband, and the vacation planning was grudgingly put off until a few days later.

I also did something that hadn't been on my to-do list. I made a point of giving my daughter a hug like she'd never felt before and thanked my lucky stars for her. It took only a minute, but I did more in that one minute than I would have done in an entire Sunday afternoon in the park with her.

> **QUICKSAND!**
>
> Values and priorities are not the same thing. Values are what matters to you, the guiding principles of your life. Priorities are the actions you deem important at any given time. Don't try to behave every day as if every value you hold is a priority, or you'll face constant ethical dilemmas.

Your Procrastinator's Oath of Effectiveness

Putting commitments and goals down on paper (or on screen) is always a good idea. When you commit to a new way of life in black and white instead of having the commitment be a vague notion floating around in your head, you increase your chances of success. To get your procrastination goals on paper, let's have a little fun and make it a very official document.

Your statement of what you want to accomplish and when and how you plan to do it, runs the risk of being like promises made during a political campaign. After a candidate is elected to office, he or she either forgets those promises or makes good on them (and we all know which they're more likely to do). You can either make good on your promises to yourself and others, or you can go on living life as a procrastinator.

> **YOU'RE NOT ALONE**
>
> They are able who think they are able.
>
> —Virgil, ancient Roman poet

By signing your name to this oath, you agree to abide by the rules of behavioral change and the bylaws and constitution of the Kingdom of Recovering Procrastinators. So if you're ready to bestow this honor upon yourself, then grab two people who can bear witness to this historic occasion, place your left hand on this book, raise your right hand, and repeat after me.

I, _____, do solemnly swear
that

- I understand procrastination is no joke, that it diminishes the quality of my life and the lives of people around me.

- Whenever I feel myself about to procrastinate, I will use the stop, look, and listen solution, no matter how tempting it may be to act on impulse.

- Before I make negative statements such as, "I just can't make myself do this," I will try as many of the 10 strategies for getting things done (as laid out in Chapter 8) as necessary until I take some positive action.

- I will not let fear, perfectionism, or other self-defeating thoughts and feelings control my life.

- I will not be overly judgmental of my behavior or put unnecessary pressure on myself. I will recognize that I'm only human and will not always be perfectly efficient—nor should I want to be.

- I will keep my priorities and goals in sight at all times.

- I will review Chapters 9 through 13 to identify specific areas of my life in which I need to stop procrastinating.

- I will make it a priority to have fun, relax, take care of myself, and connect with my family, friends, and community as often as possible.

I will faithfully execute the strategies recommended in *The Complete Idiot's Guide to Overcoming Procrastination*, and to the best of my ability, will preserve, protect, and defend the Procrastinator's Oath of Effectiveness.

_____

Signed   Date

Witnessed by:

1. _____

2. _____

Congratulations! Have the band strike up a rousing chorus of "Pomp and Circumstance." You are now inducted into the hallowed halls of recovering procrastinators.

It's Up to You

Despite all the obstacles that might be thrown your way from people, places, and things, and despite all the mind games you might inadvertently play on yourself, you are in control of your behavior. You can choose to waste time (which is allowed, even encouraged, now and then), or you can choose to make good use of it.

You can use this book as a reference tool, keeping it handy so that you can refer back to the strategies offered throughout it when you need them. Or you can give in to the "yes, buts" and say, "These techniques aren't going to work for me," and let the book gather dust on the shelf. It's entirely up to you.

As you struggle to make those choices, think about this old Saudi Arabian proverb: "If a camel once gets his nose in the tent, his body will soon follow." I want you to keep that image in mind as you try to overcome procrastination. You might feel clumsy as you stretch and strain to get things done, just like that gangly dromedary. But if you take at least one step toward your goals—merely poke your nose in the tent—and vow to stay determined, then success will follow.

The Least You Need to Know

- All the strategies in this book are useless if you don't summon up the determination to use them.
- Staying organized is an easy way to keep your procrastination-busting efforts working.
- A balanced life comes from having fun, being grateful, and staying connected to others.
- Values and priorities are not one and the same.
- Your procrastination oath is an announcement to yourself and the world that you are fed up with being a procrastinator and plan to take concrete steps toward becoming an ex-procrastinator.

Index

A

B

E